Indians of the Southern Plains

About the Book

On the vast, wide-open spaces of the southern Great Plains nomad Indian tribes created a culture based on their needs and ways of life. Then the federal government, forever pushing the Indians hither and yonder, relocated various tribes to what was then called Indian Territory, now the state of Oklahoma. As author William K. Powers reveals in this fascinating book, the Indians of the Southern Plains have been changing remarkably since the beginning of the twentieth century. Here is exciting history that tells the stories both of Indians in the past and in the present.

Standing Elk, a Ponca, was born in 1833. This photo was taken by De Lancey Gill in 1914. Standing Elk holds a pipe and beaded pipe bag. Over one shoulder is slung a bandolier made from mescal beans. In his right hand he holds a staff with horsehair pendant. (*Smithsonian Institution*)

Indians
OF THE
Southern
Plains

William K. Powers

An American Indians Then & Now Book

Earl Schenck Miers, General Editor

G. P. Putnam's Sons · New York

To *HOBART JARRETT*

Child
coll.
J
970.1
POW

Copyright © 1971 by William K. Powers
All rights reserved. Published simultaneously in
Canada by Longmans Canada Limited, Toronto.
Library of Congress Catalog Card Number: 75-147281
PRINTED IN THE UNITED STATES OF AMERICA
12 up

Acknowledgments

I would like to acknowledge the people who gave great assistance in making this book possible. Mr. and Mrs. Robert J. Voelker who first introduced me to the Southern Plains many years ago; Paul Thomas, Wichita, for his insight into the Indian people of Oklahoma; and to the late Jake Wahkinney, Comanche, his wife and family for being my gracious hosts during a number of trips to Oklahoma.

Mrs. Margaret C. Blaker, Archivist, Smithsonian Office of Anthropology, was especially helpful in selecting photographs.

My wife, Marla, and my sons, Jeffrey and Gregory, were, as usual, helpful in collecting information, and offering companionship during all our trips out west.

Finally, I thank all the Indian people in Oklahoma who were willing to put up with endless questions regarding their cultural past and present.

Aho!

W. K. P.

98229

Contents

Introduction

WHEN THE first white man crossed the Mississippi River and headed West in search of new adventures, riches, and homelands for his family, little did he suspect that he was crossing an imaginary boundary line which was in fact the threshold of a new culture.

The early pioneers, traders, and trappers had already met the Indians of the Great Lakes, the Eastern woodlands, and the Southeast. Now the adventurers were to stumble upon a new group of American Indians whose territory began at the Mississippi and extended westward to the Rocky Mountains. On the north, their land reached to the prairie provinces of Canada; to the south, the Gulf of Mexico.

The vast, wide-open spaces of this newly discovered territory were to become known as the Great Plains. The first inhabitants of this unexplored empire were to be known as the Indians of the Great Plains. These Indians shared similar customs and modes of living which differed from those of the Indians who lived east of the Mississippi. The early explorers, trappers, artists, and journalists noted these similarities in their books and diaries. Later, anthropologists were to designate this culture area as the Great Plains.

Most of the Indians of this area were nomads. They traveled great distances in search of game or warfare. As each tribe came in contact with another, there was much borrowing and trading of ideas, customs, and modes of dress. This exchange had been going on long before the white man arrived. But after his appearance on the Plains, the subsequent encroachment on tribal lands, and the ultimate consequence of open hostility ending with the Great Indian Wars, the once-free nomads were placed on reservations. It caused the Indian's life-style to change drastically. Many tribes were located on reservations which were near their original homelands. Consequently, their living standards changed little. But other tribes were forced to relocate to areas totally unfamiliar to them. Not only were these tribes removed to foreign lands, but they were relocated along with other tribes from different areas whose customs were dissimilar to the Plains culture. The proximity of the latter tribes to the original Plains Indian caused a cultural change which began to differentiate the relocated Indians from other tribes of the Great Plains.

The tribes sent to strange lands settled in what was then called Indian Territory, now the present state of Oklahoma. While the Indians of the Northern High Plains were rather isolated on separate reservations, those Indians living on the Southern Plains, about which this book is written, began to change their cultural patterns—especially since the turn of the twentieth century.

As a result of their removal to Oklahoma, where they shared a territory, later to become a state, with scores of other tribes from different regions, a natural transition took place in their ways of living that would become somewhat divorced from that of their Northern neighbors. Because of this change, another imaginary boundary line became apparent beginning approximately with World War I. The imaginary line may be drawn along the middle of the present state of Nebraska running east and west. It is with the people living south of this new boundary, the Indians of the Southern Plains, that we are concerned.

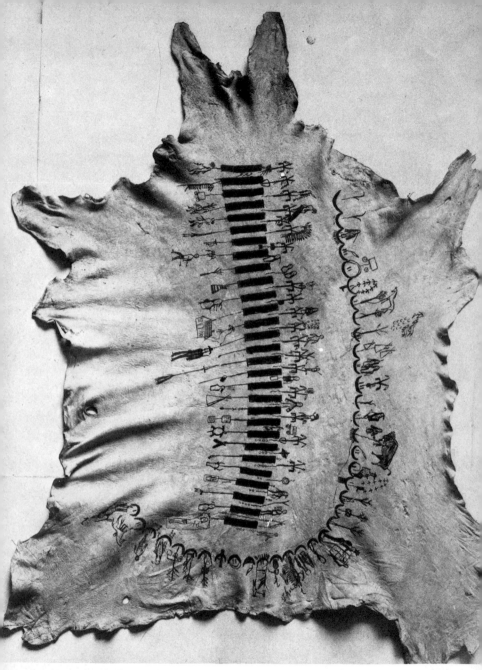

The famous Anko Monthly Count of the Kiowa. Each pictograph represents one of thirty-seven months from August, 1889, to July, 1892. This specimen was collected by James Mooney. (*Smithsonian Institution*)

1

Land of the Red Man

IT IS appropriate that a state in which 5 percent of the population is American Indian should be called "Oklahoma," a Choctaw Indian word meaning "red man." The word was coined by Allen Wright, the principal chief of the Choctaw in 1866-70, and applied to a portion of land set aside by the federal government and known as Indian Territory. This territory was to become the home of sixty-seven tribes, the first of whom began their removal to Indian Territory in the 1830's from the Southeast. They were later to be joined by tribes from the Southwest, Northern Plains and Prairies, and even the Atlantic Seaboard.

It was originally intended that Indian Territory be formed into an all-Indian state. But white men, despite treaties, began to emigrate to Oklahoma, pushing cattle drives along the old Chisholm Trail. The completion of the railroad in 1872 brought in even more whites, and in 1889 the federal government opened up the western half of the territory to homesteaders. In 1890 the western half of Indian Territory became known as Oklahoma Territory. On April 22 of that year, fifty thousand homesteaders lined up waiting for the noon deadline to rush into the territory and claim land. Those who sneaked into the territory before the noon deadline were to become known as sooners, and today the state of Oklahoma enjoys the nostalgic nickname The Sooner State, in remembrance of that occasion. The most famous run was that to Cherokee Outlet in 1893 and is sometimes remembered in history as the Cherokee Strip. A series of runs for land continued until 1901; thereafter land was sold by sealed bid.

Since 1890 the western half of Indian Territory had been known as Oklahoma Territory. Much to the opposition of the Indians living in Indian Territory, the federal government in 1887 appointed the Dawes Commission, which by 1893 began to convert lands owned by tribes through treaty into individually owned lands. In 1907 Indian Territory and Oklahoma Territory merged to become the forty-sixth state under its present name. Thus the realization of an all-Indian state was crushed, and after subsequent negotiations by the federal government, all Indian reservations in Oklahoma were abolished. However, the Indian remained living in tightly organized Indian communities.

Only a minority of Indian tribes lived in the Oklahoma area prior to the turn of the nineteenth century. These tribes—the Caddo, Comanche, Kiowa, Kiowa Apache, Lipan Apache, Tonkawa, and Wichita—were some of the first to inhabit the land of the red man. They themselves had migrated to the land of the red man from the North, Southwest, and Southeast. They were later to be joined by other tribes: the Pawnee, Southern Cheyenne, and Southern Arapaho, and various prairie tribes from Iowa, Kansas, Nebraska, Missouri, and Arkansas.

Originally the tribes that were later to be described as Southern Plains Indians inhabited Arkansas, Iowa, Kansas, parts of Louisiana, Missouri, Nebraska, Oklahoma, and Texas. These states comprise an area of nearly three-quarter million square miles. Annual rainfall averages as little as 10 inches per year in western Texas, and 50 inches a year in eastern Texas. Most of the land is rolling hills and prairies, the highest altitude being found in the western part of Texas, where the tip of the Rocky Mountains reaches 8,751 feet at Guadalupe Peak. The lowest point is found on the alluvial plain of the Mississippi River in Missouri.

The temperatures of this area are as diverse as its topography—as low as 30 degrees below zero in winter and more than 100 degrees in summer. The principal rivers of this region, the Mississippi, Missouri, Arkansas, Red River, Rio Grande, Kansas, Pecos, and Colorado, are abundant in fish. The state of Nebraska alone has more than three thousand small lakes—today, a fisherman's paradise. Virtually all species of wild game are found on the plains and prairies. Many of these animals, especially the once-abounding bison or buffalo, were the main source of food for the Indians of this region.

Most states in this area are named after tribes who originally lived there. "Iowa" comes from the name of that tribe which means "sleepy ones." "Missouri," also called Missouria, means "great muddy," the name of another tribe. "Kansas" derives its name from the Kansa, or *Kaw,* Indians. "Nebraska" is another Siouan word meaning "flat space" or "flat water." "Texas" is a variation of a Caddoan word meaning "friends," or "allies." "Arkansas" is a French corruption of the Kansa tribe.

Thus we see that in place names, as well as other aspects, the Indians of the plains have left their imprint on the land they once roamed freely.

Although there were many small tribes and bands inhabiting the area before the white man came to the Western Hemisphere, some later became extinct and other tribes formed loose confederacies. This book is primarily concerned with the principal tribes of the region: the Caddo, Comanche, Kiowa, Kiowa Apache, Iowa, Kansa, Lipan Apache, Missouri, Omaha, Osage, Oto, Pawnee, Ponca, Quapaw, Southern Cheyenne, Southern Arapaho, Tonkawa, and Wichita.

Among these tribes, a variety of languages was spoken. In all, six linguistic families, or language stocks, are represented on the Southern Plains. They are (1) the Siouan, whose members included the Iowa, Kansa, Missouri, Omaha, Osage, Oto, Ponca, and Quapaw; (2) the Caddoan, composed of the Caddo, Pawnee, and Wichita; (3) the Algonquian, made up of the Southern Cheyenne and Arapaho; (4) the Uto-Aztecan, including the Kiowa and Comanche; (5) the Athabascan, represented by the Kiowa Apache and Lipan Apache; and (6) the Tonkawan, whose sole representative here is the Tonkawa, which were composed of smaller tribes living in central Texas and western Oklahoma.

Belonging to the same language stock did not mean the tribes could understand one another. It simply meant that their languages were derived from a common source, as French and Spanish are derived from Latin. The Kiowa and Comanche could not understand each other, nor could the Lipan Apache and Kiowa Apache, the Arapaho and Cheyenne. Among the Siouan speakers, some tribes spoke a similar language, mutually intelligible to all. But even this stock was divided into two subdivisions which will be discussed later.

Before their settlement in Indian Territory, the lives of these tribes were diverse. There were four major types of dwellings used. For instance, the Kiowa, Comanche, Cheyenne, and Arapaho lived in the familiar Plains tepee. The Apache lived in their traditional wickiup, later adopting the tepee. The Omaha, Osage, and Pawnee originally lived in earth lodges resembling the dwellings of the North Dakota tribes—the Mandan, Hidatsa, and Gros Ventre. The Wichita were especially known for their immense houses and council lodges made from woven grass.

Some tribes relied entirely on hunting to provide food, clothing, and shelter, while others were part-time hunters living in well-defined villages where they raised corn, squash, and beans. With the advent of the horse, the nomads of the Southern Plains and Prairies became mobile and could move quickly across the Plains in search of game and enemies. Some tribes went as far as Mexico to raid the Spanish settlements for plunder and captives.

Some of the tribes, such as the Comanche and Apache, were warlike. The Comanche were exceptional horsemen. The name Geronimo, the famous Apache war leader, is well known even today. Other tribes, such as the Pawnee, while ferociously battling other Indians, were always peaceful to the white man. Many Pawnee served as scouts for the U.S. Army.

Religious life was equally diverse. Some tribes followed religious practices similar to Indians of the Northern High Plains, such as the annual sun dance, the sweat lodge, and vision quest. But other tribes were unique. The Pawnee, for example, at one time offered a human sacrifice during their annual Hako ceremony.

Although there is still some debate about the matter among scholars, the Tonkawa allegedly practiced cannibalism as part of their religion. In later years, the ghost dance movement reached a number of Southern Plains tribes.

While most tribes still retained their individuality after their relocation to Indian Territory, an amalgamation of traits began to take place. Because many tribes lived so close to one another, English became the common exchange of the Southern Plains. Music, dance, and costuming began to diffuse; similarities in customs became more noticeable. During the latter part of the nineteenth century a phenomenon known as the powwow, a gathering of tribe or tribes for the sole purpose of socializing with music, dance, and feasting, became an integral part of Southern Plains life. This would later influence even the Northern Plains Indians. The very word "powwow" was not indigenous to the Southern Plains. Originally the word *pauau* in Algonquian dialects referred to a special curing rite performed by a medicine man, or shaman. Whenever the medicine man performed the rites, people would gather to watch. White men witnessing the curing ceremony came to regard any gathering of people for any purpose as a powwow. The word today is even used by non-Indians to connote a picnic, gathering, or social function.

Although many tribes living on the Southern Plains were at one time hostile to each other, enmities ended with the establishment of treaties and reservations. After tribes were relocated close to one another, intertribal communication and socialization became frequent. Tribes that had retained tribal characteristics began to recognize their common denominator: They were all *Indians*.

While the Indians continued to retain many tribal values, new emphasis was placed on universal similarities: namely, their race, and especially the fact that they were *not* becoming white men even though missionaries and federal administrators tried to teach them white ways. Similarity of racial characteristics and dilemmas common to all Indians—the abrogations of treaties, the relocation to strange lands, the nearness of neighboring tribes—developed in these people the need to identify themselves in a singular manner. The movement toward merging tribal traits into a singular Indian whole is called Pan-Indianism. The movement is most evident today in the religion Peyotism, incorporated as the Native American Church, and the formation of Indian rights organizations that attempt to influence federal and state legislation on behalf of the welfare of all Indians in the United States. But it is perhaps most obvious in the artistic world of the Indian—the music, dance, and material culture which grew out of contact between tribes at intertribal events.

Out of this convergence of ideas has grown the notion of the Oklahoma Indian, although no tribe of that name technically exists.

Today it is difficult to determine what proportion of the Indians living on the Southern Plains consider themselves Indian. Through long association with whites and blacks, the rate of full-blooded Indians is on the decline. Since there is no official definition of the Indian race, many people who have less than one-half Indian blood live in a non-Indian world. By the same token, especially since the Indian Reorganization Act of 1934 which transferred Indian tribal administration to the Indians themselves, many people of less than one-half Indian descent prefer to consider themselves Indian.

As one Indian anthropologist told me, "Ever since the federal government told the people it's all right to be Indian now, Indians are coming out of the woodwork." What the anthropologist meant was that in the early reservation days the white man attempted to teach the Indians to become white men. While many Indians did in fact become absorbed into the dominant white society as ranchers, farmers, businessmen, government officials (and even a few oil tycoons), most Indians preferred to retain their native identity and live in Indian communities even after reservations were abolished. With the enactment of the Indian Reorganization Act, the Indian was theoretically free to choose whatever life —Indian or white—he wanted. The stigma of being Indian was obliterated. Thus even a few whites and blacks chose to live as what anthropologists call sociological Indian full-bloods. In other words, the way of life became more important than the degree of blood.

Today, one cannot visit Oklahoma without being constantly reminded of its rich Indian heritage. Indian names mark the counties and cities: Anadarko, Tulsa, Muskogee, Ponca City, Pawhuska, Apache, Okmulgee, Caddo, Washita, and Okfuskee. Numerous Indian celebrations take place every summer in Anadarko, Pawhuska, and various small towns. The Indian Hall of Fame and Indian City, both in Anadarko, pay homage to the Indians of yesterday and today. The Gilcrease Museum in Tulsa exhibits paintings of famous Indian artists. But most of all, one is impressed by the Indian people themselves who have survived decades of deprivation by the white man.

2

The People

OUR PURPOSE is to discuss the distinctive characteristics of only the principal tribes of the Southern Plains. Some of these tribes were largely independent, such as the Comanche, Kiowa, Cheyenne, and Arapaho, although they in turn were divided into smaller bands. Other smaller tribes, though at one time independent, formed confederacies for the purpose of protection against hostile Indians and whites. Such were the small tribes of Tawakoni, Waco, and Kichai who joined the Wichita and have been counted among that tribe for so many years that they have all but lost individual tribal identity.

Among the principal tribes some were once members of larger divisions of tribal units, such as the Cheyenne and Arapaho, who today are split into the Northern and Southern branches; the latter live in Oklahoma while their relatives dwell in Montana and Wyoming. There is still a great deal of travel between the Northern and Southern groups. Many common religious ceremonies are communally held despite the great distance that separates them. Likewise, the Comanche were once part of the Shoshoni, who lived in the Plateau area of the United States, but the Comanche separated from the Shoshoni around the turn of the eighteenth century. Despite their separation, they still share a common language.

Now let us meet the principal tribes that once ruled the Southern Plains and Prairies and investigate aspects of history and culture which made them distinct.

The Arapaho

The Arapaho, designated here as the Southern Arapaho to distinguish them from their Wyoming neighbors, are members of the Algonquian language stock—the largest Indian family of languages in the United States. "Arapaho" was coined from a Pawnee word *tirapihu*, which signifies "he buys, or trades." The Arapaho call themselves *Inuna-ina*, meaning "our people." The Northern branch calls those living in Oklahoma *Nawunena*—"Southerners." The Caddo, Comanche, and Wichita called the Arapaho "dog eaters," which referred to the tribe's particular liking of dog meat as a delicacy—a trait not uncommon among the Northern Plains tribes.

The Arapaho originally migrated from the western shore of Lake Superior and eventually inhabited Nebraska, Kansas, and parts of Colorado and Wyoming. They were traditionally associated with the Cheyenne, Kiowa, Kiowa Apache, and Comanche, who sometimes joined together to raid Spanish settlements in the Southwest. Their enemies were the Shoshoni, Ute, Navajo, and Pawnee.

In 1780 the population of the Arapaho was estimated at 3,000, and in 1881, at 2,258. In 1892, the Southern branch—the larger of the two groups—was estimated at 1,091 and is currently counted together with the Southern Cheyenne, whose combined population is nearly 4,000 in Oklahoma.

The Arapaho made treaties in Kansas with the United States in 1861 at Fort Wise, and again at Medicine Lodge in 1867. Then they were placed on reservations, the Southern Arapaho being settled on land near Canton and Colony, Oklahoma, where they currently live with their allies of old, the Cheyenne.

The Southern Arapaho were divided into five principal bands listed by the famous ethnographer James Mooney in 1892 as: (1) *Waquithi*, or "bad faces," the largest band, whose head chief was Left Hand; (2) *Aqathinena*, "pleasant men," (3) *Gawunena*, or "black people," so called because they were allegedly mixed with Blackfeet Indians; (4) *Haqihana*, "wolves," named after this band's medicine; and (5) *Sasaba-ithi*, or "lookouts."

The Arapaho, always noted for being a particularly religious people, participated in the annual sun dance when living on the Northern Plains. They also took readily to the ghost dance religion which was popular among many Northern and Southern Plains tribes during the late 1880's.

Northern and Southern Arapaho still observe their closeness as a tribe and make frequent visits to one another's communities to participate in religious ceremonies and social events. Many of the Southern Arapaho travel to Wyoming for the summer powwows sponsored by the Northern Arapaho and are always warmly received by their relatives with elaborate ceremonies and gifts. Today the Southern Arapaho also are hosts at their own powwows in the summer and participate enthusiastically in all Oklahoma Indian events.

The Caddo

The Caddo are the principal members of the Caddoan linguistic family, which also includes the Wichita, Kichai, Pawnee, and Arikara, the latter of which live in North Dakota.

The Caddo were first discovered by LaSalle in 1686-87, although one of their numerous affiliate tribes, the Nadako, were mentioned by DeSoto in 1540. In the early days various experts claim that there were from 12 to 25 Caddoan tribes, which were in turn divided into three main confederacies, the *Kadohadacho* ("real chiefs") or Caddo proper, from which the tribal name is derived; the *Hasinai*, the Caddo name for the confederacy meaning "our people"; and the Wichita. The French, Kiowa, Cheyenne, and Arapaho called them "pierced noses" after their custom of boring their nose for the purpose of inserting a ring. In 1896, Mooney listed the following 12 Caddoan tribes: (1) *Kadohadacho*, (2) *Hainai*, (3) *Anadarko*, (4) *Nabedache*, (5) *Nacogdoches*, (6) *Natchitoches*, (7) *Yatasi*, (8) *Adai*, (9) *Eyeish*, (10) *Nakanawan*, (11) *Imaha*, probably a small band of Quapaw, and (12) *Yowani*, a band of Choctaw that lived with the Caddo. Other smaller tribes eventually became extinct.

The Caddo originally lived on the lower Red River in Louisiana, and in parts of southwestern Arkansas and northeastern Texas, suggesting a westward expansion from the Southeast. They originally lived in thatched houses similar to those of the Wichita and were agriculturists, raising large crops of corn, pumpkins, and melons, and also manufacturing salt. When they moved onto the Plains, they readily adapted to a hunter's way of life and became excellent horsemen. They were also known as great traders and were proficient in the Indian sign language.

A Caddo Indian, Tall Man. Photo by Wells Sawyer, 1898. (*Smithsonian Institution*)

Small in size and darker than their neighbors on the Plains, the Caddo were congenial and never waged war against the United States, though they were noted for bravery in battles against the Osage and the Choctaw. The Caddo signed a treaty with the United States in 1835 and were moved to the Brazos River in Texas. In 1859 they moved to Indian Territory. During the Civil War, the Caddo Battalion served as scouts for the Confederacy and was one of the last Confederate forces to surrender in July, 1865.

The population of the Caddo proper was estimated at 2,000 in 1700, reaching an all-time low of 800 in 1805. Numbers increased during reservation days, and the population is currently estimated at 1,670.

Originally the Caddo were divided into ten clans comprising the Bear, Wolf, Buffalo, Beaver, Eagle, Raccoon, Crow, Thunder, Panther, and Sun. The Bear clan was the most numerous. The Buffalo clan was sometimes called the Alligator clan. It was a strict custom of the Caddo that no member kill an animal which served as the totem of his clan. One exception was the eagle, which might be killed for its feathers by a hunter especially initiated for that purpose.

The Caddo currently live in Caddo County, Oklahoma, near the town of Binger and sponsor an annual powwow. The town of Anadarko, Oklahoma, is named after the *Nadako* division of Caddo and is translated "place of honey."

The Cheyenne

The Southern Cheyenne, as they have been called since their removal to Indian Territory, are Algonquian speakers who have been traditionally linked with the Southern Arapaho in Oklahoma. Like their Arapaho neighbors, another branch of the Cheyenne lives on the Northern Plains in the present state of Montana.

In the mid-seventeenth century the Cheyenne lived in the Great Lakes region in earth lodges, where they tended gardens of corn, squash, and beans. During the latter part of the seventeenth century they migrated to the Plains, where they were friendly with the tribes living on the upper Missouri. They received horses around 1760 and adapted easily to the tepee-dwelling, buffalo-hunting life of the plains Indian.

As Plains Indians, they occupied western Montana, eastern Wyoming, northwestern Nebraska, and parts of Colorado, where they allied themselves with the Sioux and the Arapaho fighting against the Kiowa, Crow, Pawnee, and Comanche.

The name "Cheyenne" comes from the Sioux word *sahiyela* meaning "alien speakers." The Cheyenne call themselves *Tsistsista* meaning "the people." The Oklahoma Cheyennes are called by their northern relatives *Sowania*, "Southerners." Various experts report that the Cheyenne were divided into anywhere from 4 to 13 bands—the discrepancy lying in the fact that some bands became extinct, or split to form new bands.

One example is the Dog Soldiers, originally a warrior society which later became a full-fledged Cheyenne band. The original 4 bands were comprised of the Aorta, Hairy Men, Dog Men, and Eaters. At a later date, a separate division, the *Sutaio*, who speak a distinct dialect, became incorporated into the Cheyenne camp circle. In 1896, Mooney reported 11 bands, stating that the Hairy Men band was often used to designate all Southern Cheyenne, while the Eaters band was used to signify the Northern Cheyenne. A later expert states that 2 bands derived from the Dog Men and 3 from the Hairy Men. With the addition of the *Sutaio*, the Cheyenne camp then had 10 bands. Later some of the older bands split, increasing the total number to 13. The entire Cheyenne tribe was governed by a council of 44 chiefs of whom 4 were designated head chiefs. The Cheyenne are particularly known for their sophisticated political and legal institutions.

In 1780, the Cheyenne were estimated at 3,500. The Northern and Southern groups did not divide until 1833, the Southern Cheyenne staying near their original homeland in Colorado. From 1857 to 1879 the Cheyenne were the target of white antagonism. In 1864, a Cheyenne camp was annihilated by Colonel J. M. Chivington in the historic Sand Creek Massacre. In 1868, the Cheyenne chief Black Kettle was killed by troops under the command of George Armstrong Custer in the famous Battle of the Washita. Subsequently, both Northern and Southern Cheyenne were commanded to report to the Southern Cheyenne Reservation in Oklahoma.

Finding it impossible to live in the new country, the Cheyenne chiefs Dull Knife and Little Wolf led 300 Northern Cheyenne back to their High Plains homeland. U.S. troops harassed the tiny, straggling band, and after they reached their homeland, they were ordered to return to the hated Southern land. In January, 1879, they began a forced march back to Oklahoma through the biting cold of the winter. Unable to withstand the rigors of the forced march, they rebelled against the soldiers. However, weakened from the harsh climate and lack of food, they were easily beaten by government troops. Sixty-four Cheyenne were killed on that march and 78 captured; the rest escaped to the North where their descendants now live on the Tongue River Reservation in Montana.

Like the Arapaho, the Cheyenne were particularly

religious and participated in the sun dance, ghost dance, and a rite called the sacred arrow renewal.

The Southern Cheyenne today live near the towns of Clinton, El Reno, Concho, Watonga, and Canton, Oklahoma. Their population has remained fairly constant since 1892, when they numbered slightly more than 2,000. Today they are counted along with the Arapaho.

The Comanche

Sometimes referred to as the most skillful horsemen of the Southern Plains, the Comanche are ancient split-offs of the Shoshoni tribe and members of the Shoshonean branch of the Uto-Aztecan linguistic family. They are one of the most widely known tribes to Indian and non-Indian alike.

The Comanche, who call themselves *Numinu*, or "the people," originally lived in the Rocky Mountains as part of the Shoshoni tribe. There they hunted and fished for their livelihood and lived a nomadic life. Around 1700 they separated from the Shoshoni and migrated southward to the North Platte River in Nebraska and by 1805 were warring with virtually every tribe with which they came in contact.

Medium in height and heavyset, the fearless Comanche fought with the Sioux in their original homelands, and later in their forays across Oklahoma and Texas with the Kiowa, Caddo, Apache, and Osage, sweeping far into Spanish territory where they raided settlements in search of booty and captives. It is probably from the Spanish that they received their popular name. Experts speculate that "Comanche" comes from the Spanish words *camino ancho*, signifying "broad trail"—the ex-

A Comanche named Ako carries a straight-up fan made of eagle feathers in his left hand and an umbrella in his right. Photographed by Hutchins and Lanney, 1892. (*Smithsonian Institution*)

tensive range of land the Comanche traveled during war and hunting expeditions.

One particularly exaggerated population figure places them at 20,000 in 1851. A more realistic figure places them at 2,538 in 1869, and 2,700 in 1950. Today they are currently counted among the Kiowa and Apache at a combined population of nearly 10,000.

As is true of all nomadic hunters, the Comanche were divided into bands. Since the bands were not stable, some dividing into splinter groups, others merging into larger ones, it is difficult to estimate precisely how many Comanche bands actually existed throughout history. As late as 1933, Comanche could recall the names of 13 bands, but often more than one name was used for a band, so no exact figure can be determined. It is known, however, that at least 5 bands were always prominent: the *Kwahadi*, or "Antelope Band"; (2) *Penateka*, or "Honey Eaters"; (3) the *Nokoni*, or "Wanderers," whose famous head chief was Quanah Parker; (4) *Yamparika*, or "Yampa Eaters" ("yampa," which the Comanches call *yap*, is a potatolike root); and (5) *Kotsoteka*, "Buffalo Eaters." In 1896, Mooney also listed 5 extinct bands.

Although the Comanche made their first treaty with the United States in 1835, unrest and hostility broke out chiefly because of the annexation of Texas in 1845 and the Gold Rush of 1849. The Comanche were constantly at war with the Texans and Mexicans along the Santa Fe Trail. In 1864 Kit Carson led federal troops against the Comanche, who by this time had ended their hostilities with many tribal enemies in order to unite against the common white foe. Despite the efforts of Carson and the U.S. Army, the Comanche remained undefeated in their skirmishes with federal troops. It was not until after signing the Medicine Lodge Treaty in 1867 that the Comanche were persuaded to move to a reservation between the Washita and Red rivers in southwestern Oklahoma. They continued to war against other tribes and whites until the last uprising on the Southern Plains in 1874-75 when, greatly weakened by war and disease, they finally settled near Fort Sill.

The Comanche, still a proud tribe, currently live near the towns of Anadarko, Fort Cobb, Carnegie, Apache, Mountain View, Gotebo, Hobart, Lawton, Cache, and Walters, Oklahoma.

The Iowa

There is historical evidence that the Iowa tribe, along with the Oto and Missouri tribes, were originally members of the Winnebago and lived in the Great Lakes region. The Iowa separated from the Winnebago and migrated southwestward through Minnesota, Iowa, Illinois, Missouri, and Kansas. Whites called the tribe "Iowa," a corruption of a Siouan word meaning "sleepy." But they called themselves *Pahoja*, meaning "gray blankets," probably alluding to their use of white trade blankets which became discolored from use. They belonged to the Chiwere division of the Siouan linguistic family and shared a dialect close to their neighbors', the Oto and the Missouri.

Always a relatively small tribe, the Iowa numbered 1,100 in 1760; 800 in 1804; 470 in 1843; 118 in 1950; and currently 350. The great decrease in numbers was due to a smallpox epidemic in 1803.

The Iowa were great traders and agriculturists, cultivating corn, beans, and squash, and trading in beaver, otter, raccoon, deer, and bear skins. They manufactured stone pipes of catlinite obtained from the great pipestone quarry in Minnesota.

An Iowa Indian named Standing on the Prairie, also known as John Grant, wears an elaborate otter fur turban. Photographed by De Lancey Gill, 1900. (*Smithsonian Institution*)

The Iowa camp was divided into two half circles, each of which was inhabited by four groups of related families. In the first half were the Black Bear, Wolf, Eagle, and Thunder Being. The second half circle was occupied by the Beaver, Pigeon, Buffalo, and Snake.

The Iowa apparently warred little with other tribes, except for the Sioux, when they lived in Minnesota. They conducted friendly trade with the white man. They ceded all their lands to the whites in 1824 and were assigned a reservation in northeastern Kansas in 1836. Later they were moved to Oklahoma where they now live in the vicinity of the town of Perkins. A few still live in Kansas.

The Kansa

The Kansa (Kanze), or *Kaw* Indians, received their name from the Osage who called them *Konce* referring to "wind" or "southwind people." The state of Kansas is named after them. They are one of the five Dhegiha-speaking people of the Siouan linguistic family sharing a dialect with the Osage, Omaha, Ponca, and Quapaw.

The Kansa were a warlike tribe hostile to the Cheyenne and the Pawnee from whom they learned to build earth lodges. The Kansa also used temporary dwellings when on the buffalo hunt. Their original home was in the vicinity of Topeka.

They were divided into three bands: the *Gaholi*, or "Creek" band under Chief Nopauwoi; the *Monhazuli* or "Yellow cutbank" band, under Chief Aligawahu; and *Bigiu*, or "Nickel" band (so called because they were first to receive five-cent pieces) under Chief Wacunge. The three bands were in turn divided into numerous subdivisions. The tribe was governed by the

Wah-shun-gah, a Kansa chief, is at the right; the other man is unidentified. Photo by C. M. Bell, 1880. (*Smithsonian Institution*)

leaders of the five most important clans and the office was hereditary. In addition to hereditary chiefs, other chiefs might be chosen by a common council, or by the hereditary chiefs themselves without the consent of the people.

In the old days prominent warriors were tattooed by professionals who owned special tattooing bundles. If a man was consistently brave in battle, he might also have the privilege of having his wife tattooed. A round spot was made on her forehead between the eyes. Her arms and wrists might also be tattooed. The woman of a prominent warrior might also wear a ring pierced through her nose.

The population of the Kansa was 1,700 in 1850. War and disease caused their numbers to dwindle to 600. The remnants of the Kansa currently live in Kay County, Oklahoma.

The Kiowa

One of the largest and most popular tribes of the Southern Plains, the Kiowa, like their neighbors, the Comanche, originally migrated to the Southern Plains from western Montana where they were located at the source of the Yellowstone and Missouri rivers. In their original homeland they made an alliance with the Crow Indians which is still cherished. Crow and Kiowa make frequent trips to each other's homes today. The name "Kiowa" comes from their own tribal designation *Kaigwu*, meaning "the people."

After receiving horses, the Kiowa moved to the Black Hills of South Dakota until driven off by the Sioux and Cheyenne. They left the Black Hills at the turn of the nineteenth century and moved to western Kansas and eastern Colorado, and eventually to Oklahoma. They are members of the Kiowan branch of the Uto-Aztecan linguistic family.

In their new home they first fought the Comanche, then later allied with them. Their traditional enemies were the Caddo, Tonkawa, Ute, Osage, Navajo, and some Apache tribes. They were friendly to the Wichita, Kicahi, Tawakoni, and Waco.

Their population, first listed in 1875, was 1,070. In the 1950's their numbers reached 3,000, despite an epidemic of measles in 1892 which greatly reduced their size. Today they are counted with the Comanche and the Apache and their combined population is almost 10,000.

The Kiowa were divided into six bands, each with its own chief, and camped according to a specific circular plan when coming together for ceremonies and meetings. The six bands were (1) the *Kata*, or "Biters"; (2) the *Kogui*, or "Elks"; (3) the *Kaigwu*, or Kiowa proper; (4) the *Kingep*, or "Big Shields"; (5) the *Semat*, "Thieves," or Kiowa Apache, a separate small tribe that was closely allied with the Kiowa and allowed to camp in the circle; and (6) *Sindiyuis*, or "Sindi's Children," named after Sindi, the mythical hero of the Kiowa. This band was also known as the *Kongtalyui*, or "Black Boys." A seventh band, the *Kuato*, or "pulling up" band, was exterminated by the Sioux.

The Kiowa were typical Plains dwellers, living in tepees and hunting buffalo on horseback. They participated in the sun dance, but, unlike their northern neighbors, did not participate in torture of the dancers. The last sun dance was held in 1891. They also took part in the ghost dance of the latter part of the nineteenth century.

They were considered by the whites and many Indians to be one of the most hostile and adventurous of all Southern Plains tribes, raiding far into Texas and Mexico against the whites. In 1867 they signed the Medicine Lodge Treaty and the next year were forced to live on a reservation at Fort Sill, Oklahoma. But even after being placed on reservations, the Kiowa continued to go on the warpath against whites and Indians. Along with their Comanche allies, they took part in the fight at Adobe Walls, Texas. Among their great leaders were Satanta, Satank, Kicking Bird, Big Tree, and Lone Wolf. In 1875, after continual harassment by United States troops, the Kiowa surrendered at Fort Sill. They currently live in the vicinity of Carnegie, Oklahoma.

Today the Kiowa are considered a particularly creative people and excel in fine craftwork. Some of the leading singers who participate in Oklahoma ceremonies are Kiowa. The tribe has also been active in the American Indian Exposition, held each year at Anadarko, Oklahoma, and presents outstanding performers at Indian City, U.S.A., located near Anadarko.

The Kiowa have produced a number of artists well known throughout the Southwest and the Plains, including Stephen Mopope, Monroe Tsatoke, Jack Hokeah, and Spencer Asah.

The Kiowa are particularly proud of their tribal traditions and not long ago reinstated the Kiowa Black Legging Society, a military society whose members are veterans of World Wars I and II, Korea, and Vietnam.

The tribe was particularly honored in 1969, when one of its members, Dr. N. Scott Momaday, received the Pulitzer Prize for fiction.

The Kiowa Apache

As mentioned previously, the Kiowa Apache became

an integral part of the Kiowa tribe, and their history and customs parallel the latter since they migrated south with the Kiowa.

The Kiowa Apache are Athabascan speakers, linguistically related to the Apaches of the Southwest, though there was no intercourse between the two groups. They call themselves *Nadiish dena*, meaning "our people." Although they spent most of their history occupying an important place in the Kiowa camp circle, the two tribes spoke completely different languages.

In 1805 Lewis and Clark estimated their population at 300. There were 344 in 1875 when they surrendered along with the Kiowa at Fort Sill, and only 194 in 1924. Current estimates place them at about 400. However, they are officially counted with the Kiowa, Comanche, and Apache. The Kiowa Apache now live in Fort Cobb and Apache, Oklahoma.

A distinguished Kiowa Apache, Tennyson Berry, served as director of the American Indian Exposition in Anadarko.

The Lipan and Chiricahua Apache

Although the Apache tribe is generally associated with the Southwestern United States, namely Arizona and New Mexico, some of the Eastern Apache were full-fledged members of the Southern Plains. While the majority of Apache continue to live in Arizona and New Mexico, two groups—the Lipan and some of the *Chiricahua*—dwelt in the marginal area of New Mexico and Colorado and later moved onto the Texas and Oklahoma Plains. The *Chiricahua* are particularly well known in American history because of one of their prominent leaders, a great and cunning warrior whose very name caused the flesh to tingle during the savage wars of the West: Geronimo.

The Lipan Apache, an offshoot of the Jicarilla Apache, called themselves *Tcicihi*, "people of the forest." "Lipan" is derived from the Apache *Ipa*, a personal name, and *n'de*, meaning "people." The latter term is also the tribal name of the Navajo, to whom the Apache are related. All are members of the Athabascan linguistic family. *Chiricahua* is Apache for "great mountain," in keeping with the tribe's practice of naming bands and subdivisions after natural phenomena. "Apache" is probably an adaptation of the Zuni word *apachu*, meaning "enemies," which they applied to the Navajo.

The Lipan, who separated from the Jicarilla in the seventeenth century, moved onto the Oklahoma and Texas Plains where they warred against the Comanche. Although most Apache tribes were hostile to the United States and Mexico, the Lipan aided the Spanish against other Apache war parties. The Lipan had a population of possibly 8,000 in the mid-eighteenth century. However, wars and disease in Texas caused them to be almost annihilated. Currently they number about 150 and are merged with the Kiowa Apache in Fort Sill and with the Tonkawa in Oakland, Oklahoma.

The Eastern Apache were tepee dwellers and buffalo hunters. In mountainous regions they also lived in small huts called wickiups. The Spanish who first came in contact with Apache villages in the mid-sixteenth century referred to the villages as *rancherias*, and the total land of the Apache as *Apacheria*.

Although the Eastern Apache raised havoc with the Spanish, they were relatively at peace with the Americans until Texans began encroaching upon Mexican territory. Cochise, another well-known leader of the

Chiricahua, was friendly with the United States until he was arrested by federal troops when visiting a camp under a flag of truce. Feeling betrayed, he and the other *Chiricahua* waged war against the United States with such violence that they soon became known as the Wild Apache. Despite their small numbers, the Apache were so able in raids by a few warriors on white settlements that word spread that great numbers of Apaches were waging war. Federal forces under the command of Kit Carson were finally deployed to crush the strength of the few Apache.

Although the Apache wanted to return home to the Southwest, the remnants of the Lipan and *Chiricahua* were eventually placed on reservations in Oklahoma. After a brief period of time they were allowed to return home. Their Arizona reservation was ultimately invaded by coal miners and water rights were withheld from the Apache, leading to a ten-year war in which Geronimo and other Apache leaders raided white settlements. The war continued until General Nelson A. Miles finally overpowered Geronimo and his band and sent them to Fort Marion, Florida, in exile. Many died in the new environment. Finally the government allowed the prisoners of war to return to Fort Sill, Oklahoma, where they remained as prisoners until 1913. Geronimo joined Pawnee Bill's Wild West Show and eventually died of pneumonia in 1909. He was buried in the cemetery at Cache Creek where a monument has been erected.

The remnants of the *Chiricahua* currently live in Apache, Oklahoma, and number about 200.

The Omaha

The Omaha are one of the five Dhegiha speakers of

the Siouan linguistic family and share a dialect common with the Kansa, Osage, Ponca, and Quapaw. The name "Omaha" means "going against the wind," or "upstream people." At one time they were the largest tribe in Nebraska, numbering 1,900 in 1829, and currently 2,700. Their population rose sharply after they had been reduced to 300 after an epidemic of smallpox in 1802.

Their original homes were in the Southeast, but like the other Siouan groups they migrated to the Great Lakes region. There they warred with the Sioux and were forced into South Dakota and Nebraska.

The Omaha lived in earth lodges during most of the year, but also used tepees and, occasionally, bark lodges. Pottery was made before 1850, but became a lost art after that period. Men were allowed to marry more than one woman, but no more than three. Like the Iowa, the Omaha were divided into half tribes, each composed of several related groups. The *Hangashenu* half tribe was divided into the (1) *Wezhinshte*, (2) *Inkesabe*, (3) *Hanga*, (4) *Dhatada*, and (5) *Kanze*. The *Inshtasanda* half tribe consisted of (1) *Mandhinkagaghe*, (2) *Tesinde*, (3) *Tapa*, (4) *Ingdhezhide*, and (5) *Inshtasanda*.

The Omaha made treaties with the United States in 1830 and 1836, and in 1854 ceded all of their land west of the Missouri, retaining a small portion near the Iowa bluffs for their reservation. In 1865 they sold part of their reservation to the United States to be used as a reservation for the Winnebago. Today, the Omaha live near the town of Macy, Nebraska, not many miles from the Nebraska Winnebago. The Omaha also live in communities in Omaha, and Lincoln, Nebraska. They make frequent trips south to Oklahoma to participate in Indian programs, as well as north into South Dakota

An unidentified Omaha Indian taken by F. N. Bentley in Nebraska around 1907. His turban is decorated with ribbon appliqué, beads, and ermine skins. His leggings are of a type called "front seam," typical of Southern Plains design. (*Smithsonian Institution*)

to attend Sioux celebrations. They are also frequent guests of the Winnebago at their annual celebration in Winnebago, Nebraska.

The Osage

The image of the wealthy Indian, driving expensive automobiles until they run out of gas to then trade them in for others, is largely provided by the Osage, one of the more fortunate Indian tribes in the entire United States. It is a little-known fact that during the first half of the twentieth century, the Osage were the *wealthiest nation per capita in the world*, receiving some $300,-000,000 in oil and gas royalties which was apportioned among something over 2,000 members of the tribe!

Their fortune—which they received by accident—was largely publicized, thus giving many whites the idea that all Indians in Oklahoma are wealthy. This in fact is far from reality. Even the Osage went through a period in which they lost almost 50 percent of their tribe because of inadequate food, clothing, and medicine, and the hardships of living in a barren land which was largely apportioned to them as their reservation in order to get them out of the way. The surface of the land, however, was resting on a not too barren well of natural resources—oil! Through careful management, the Osage tribe was able to capitalize on the resources, being careful to permit all members to share in the newfound riches.

The Osage are another member of the Dhegiha-speaking Siouans who migrated from the Carolinas and Virginia to the Great Lakes along with the Kansa, Omaha, Ponca, and Quapaw, crossing the Mississippi River to reside on the Osage River in southwestern Missouri and southeastern Kansas. Hunting, and war

A young Osage Indian girl wearing a blanket with elaborate
appliqué ribbon work. (*Smithsonian Institution*)

against the Caddoan tribes, the Cherokee, Kiowa, and Comanche, led them to transverse even a wider territory, including Arkansas and Oklahoma.

The word "Osage" is a French corruption of their own tribal designation *Wajaje*, which has been defined in a number of ways. Some experts claim that the term is related to the Omaha *wabaji*, meaning "messenger"; others think that it means "snake." John Joseph Mathews, an Osage and a graduate of Oxford University, England, in his comprehensive study of his own tribe, *The Osages—Children of the Middle Waters*, defines the word as "name givers," referring to the mythical beings who in Osage cosmology gave names to all the people and objects of the earth.

The tribe was divided into two bands, the *Pahatsi*, or "Great Osage," and *Utsehta*, or "Little Osage." The Osage first signed a treaty with the United States in 1808, moving to Kansas. In another treaty in 1825 they ceded all lands to the United States and moved to northern Oklahoma. During the Civil War the Great Osage served with the Confederate Army while the Little Osage aligned themselves with the North, thus causing great factionalism between the two bands. In 1872, the entire tribe was finally moved to their present reservation centering around the town of Pawhuska, named after one of their great chiefs.

The Osage have remained a relatively large tribe despite their heavy losses when they were placed on the reservation. Lewis and Clark estimated their numbers at 6,500 in 1805. In 1950, they numbered 4,972, and in 1967, 5,307. They are presently located near the towns of Pawhuska, Gray Horse, and Hominy, Oklahoma.

The Osage command a great deal of respect from other tribes on the Southern Plains because of their exactness in keeping the traditions of the old people.

Each year the tribe sponsors celebrations in their communities when they conduct straight dances, or old-time dances reminiscent of the war and hunting days. The term "straight dance" is used to differentiate the dance from the "fancy war dance," which is performed at intertribal gatherings by most of the Oklahoma tribes as well as tribes outside the state. In the straight dance, primarily performed by men who dance in a very reserved and dignified manner, there is a great deal of Indian protocol observed. Only old-time songs are sung; certain men are selected to dance as whip men and tail men—special honorific roles in the straight dance. There is much ceremony, gift giving, and an outstanding display of fine costuming evident at the Osage celebrations.

Due to their careful management of money, many Osage are prominent businessmen in Oklahoma. Others, in addition to John Joseph Mathews, have achieved fame. The distinguished soloist of the Ballet Russe de Monte Carlo, Maria Tallchief, is an Osage.

The Oto-Missouri

Once a single tribe which separated after a dispute between leaders into two distinct tribes, both Chiwere speakers of the Siouan linguistic family, the Oto and Missouri reaffiliated into one tribe after the turn of the nineteenth century. At that time the Missouri had been badly beaten by the Sac and Fox and were forced to take up residence with the Osage, Kansa, and Oto. In 1829 the Missouri were again defeated by the Osage and later were forced to join the Iowa and Oto. Since 1905, the Missouri have been officially classified with the Oto. Thus the dual designation.

"Oto," sometimes spelled Otoe, comes from the

Big Black Bear, an Oto-Missouri Indian, wears a bear claw necklace and trade silver earrings. Photographed around 1884. (*Smithsonian Institution*)

Ponca word *Wathodahan*, signifying "lechers." "Missouri" is from the Illini (after which Illinois is named) tribal word for "great muddy," by which the Missouri River was known. The Missouri call themselves *Niutachi*, or "those that arrive at the mouth (of the river)."

The Oto and Missouri were primarily agriculturists who, along with the Winnebago, migrated from the Southeast to the Great Lakes region. There they separated to travel south in search of new lands and buffalo. In 1817 they were living in a number of villages located on the Platte River in Nebraska. They signed treaties with the United States in 1817, 1825, and, between 1830 and 1854, a number of treaties ceding their land to the federal government. They were then established on a reservation on the Kansas-Nebraska line. They were moved to Indian Territory in 1881.

There were an estimated 931 Oto-Missouri in 1843, and following the fate of their neighboring tribes, they were reduced to 377 in 1891 because of epidemics. They numbered 930 in 1950, and currently have a combined population of approximately 1,000.

The Oto-Missouri currently live in Noble County, Oklahoma, and are sponsors of an annual powwow at Red Rock. Like the Osage, the Oto-Missouri are active in the traditional straight dances and travel from town to town to engage in a number of intertribal events. Over the years, the Oto-Missouri have produced a number of outstanding fancy dancers who have won championship dance contests at the American Indian Exposition in Anadarko, as well as at smaller powwows. Despite being few in number, the Oto-Missouri are still predominantly full-blooded Indians.

The Pawnee

The Pawnee, who once inhabited much of Kansas

and Nebraska, were renowned as fierce warriors in their campaigns against the Sioux, Osage, and other Siouan-speaking groups which surrounded them. However, they are remembered as never having engaged in hostilities against the federal government and did, in fact, serve as scouts for the U.S. Army.

These Caddoan speakers called themselves *Chahiksichahiks*, or "men of men." They were divided into four bands comprised of the *Chaui*, or "Grand Pawnee"; the *Kitkehahki*, or "Republican"; the *Pitahauirata*, or "tappage"; and the *Skidi*, or "Wolf." The word "Pawnee" probably comes from the word *pariki*, meaning "horn," which refers to a peculiar way in which the Pawnee men wore their hair. They shaved their heads and left a narrow strip of hair down the center of their head resembling a horn. Some experts believe the word may also be a Choctaw word, *pana*, which refers to the scalp lock.

The Western Sioux called the Pawnee *Scili*, a corruption of their own term, *Skidi*. The relatives of the Pawnee on the Northern Plains, the Arikara, were called *Palani*, evidently a corruption of the tribal designation.

The Sioux, who were constantly engaged in war with the Pawnee in the early days, had great respect for the Pawnee's use of the bow and arrow in battle. One Sioux told me that the Pawnee were capable of shooting their arrows in such a manner "that arrows would curve right up under your shield and wound you." While this seems highly unlikely, it at least shows the degree of respect the Sioux had for their traditional enemy's prowess in battle.

The Pawnee, who are believed to have migrated with other Caddoan speakers from the Southeast, lived in earth lodges and raised corn, beans, pumpkins, and squash, besides hunting buffalo. They were particularly noted for their rich religious way of life. They worshiped the Morning Star, to whom they offered a human sacrifice—a maiden captured from another tribe. The practice of sacrifice was eventually ended by

These Pawnee Indians were photographed beside an earth lodge around 1868. Their names, from left to right, were: Stopped with the Horse, Humane Chief, As a Dog but yet a Chief, Good Chief, Difficult Chief. (*Smithsonian Institution*)

one of their great chiefs, Petalesharo. They had numerous bundle societies and participated in one annual event called the Hako, which will be discussed later. The sacred bundles were often referred to as *atira*, or "mother." Two ears of corn were kept in each bundle, which was also sometimes called *chuharipiru*, or "wrapped up rainstorm." The name alluded to the importance the Pawnee gave to rain and the west where thunder supposedly dwelled.

The *Skidi* were the largest and most important of the four bands. The band was divided into thirteen villages, each having its own sacred bundle. All spoke an identical language which differed dialectically from the other three divisions. The *Pitahauirata* were divided into two villages, the *Kawarakis* and *Pitahauirat*. The *Chaui* and *Kitkehahki* each resided in a single village. A man's lineage was traced through his mother, and the women never left the village in which they were born. If a man married a woman from another village, he had to go to her village to live and their children would be considered members of the wife's residence. However, marrying outside one's village was frowned upon and could not be accomplished without the special consent of the village headmen. The headmen, or chiefs, were always custodians of the sacred bundles of their respective villages.

The Pawnee also participated in the sun dance, which they claimed they learned from the Arikara of North Dakota. Their sun dance resembled the ceremony of most other tribes in which the main participants inserted pegs of wood into the fleshy part of the chest, which were attached by thong to a pole. Participants danced until the flesh tore loose.

The Pawnee also participated in the ghost dance, which was started by a Paiute Indian in Nevada in the latter part of the nineteenth century and spread rapidly among many tribes of the Northern and Southern Plains.

The Pawnee once were a large tribe estimated at 10,000 in 1838, despite the fact that in 1831 smallpox decimated almost half the tribe. In 1849 cholera killed more than 1,000. Weakened greatly by disease, drought, and the decimation of the buffalo, the Pawnee were reduced to less than 3,000 in 1928. There are approximately that number now living near Pawhuska, Oklahoma, where they resettled after their removal to Indian Territory in 1875-76.

Today, the Pawnee sponsor one of the most popular annual events in Oklahoma called the Pawnee Indian Homecoming, which is held over the Fourth of July holidays. Tribes travel from all parts of Oklahoma as well as neighboring states to participate in this event.

Many early traditions of the Pawnee were recorded by a member of their tribe, James Murie, who became a leading anthropologist for the American Museum of Natural History and Bureau of American Ethnology.

The Ponca

The Ponca, along with the Osage, Kansa, Omaha, and Quapaw—all Dhegiha speakers of the Siouan linguistic family—migrated from the Southeast to the Plains area, taking up residence in southern South Dakota and northeastern Nebraska. Considered an offshoot of the Omaha tribe, they lived in two villages, the Gray Blanket and Fish Smell, on the prairies.

Although the word "Ponca" is used by the tribe itself as well as the other Siouan speakers to designate the Omaha split-off, no one—not even the Ponca—remembers what the word means. There has been some conjec-

The famous Ponca chief, White Eagle, after whom an Oklahoma community is named. The photo was taken at some time before 1877. (*Smithsonian Institution*)

ture that it is related to the Siouan word *Pahonga*, meaning "sacred head," but no true evidence exists. Like other Siouan tribes, the Ponca were divided into two half tribes containing seven (some experts say eight) clans. The two half tribes were called the *Wajaje* (the same name used by the related Osage to designate their own tribe) and *Tshiju*. When the clans camped in the village circle, each was assigned a specific location.

The Ponca lived in earth lodges and were agriculturists raising the traditional crop of corn, beans, squash, and pumpkins. Too, they were buffalo hunters and used small tepees when on the hunt. They also provided their livelihood by fishing.

Being on the periphery of Sioux country, they first allied with them to fight against the Pawnee, but most of the time they were at odds with the Sioux. Later, the Ponca became closely affiliated with the Eastern Sioux, a friendship which they still respect today.

Like the Cheyenne, the Ponca were removed to Indian Territory, but some refused to go to the southern country. There was, therefore, a split in the tribe. Today we may speak of the Northern and Southern Ponca, although the majority live in Oklahoma around the towns of Ponca City and White Eagle. The latter town was named after the head chief of the Ponca who held his position for fifty years. The removal of the Ponca to Indian Territory in 1877 was a terrible ordeal because of heavy rains and disease; it has been called, along with other such forced marches of tribes from their original homelands to new lands, the Ponca Trail of Tears.

There was little change in population after 1876 when the Ponca were estimated at 730. Today they number a little over 1,000.

Although the Ponca live in the vicinity of a number of different tribes in Oklahoma and participate in many intertribal events, they are especially known for their tendency to cling to many of the traditional Indian ways of life. In the mid-fifties they reorganized one of their old dancing societies called the *Hedushka* (pronounced Hay-THOO-shkah with the "th" as in "the") complete with ceremonies, costumes, ritual paraphernalia, and, most of all, the traditional songs. When it comes to traditional Indian singing, the Ponca are exceeded by none. They are often asked to travel far to provide the singing for traditional powwows, especially where there is a great deal of straight dancing. Names like Sylvester Warrior, Albert Waters, and Lamont Brown, though unknown to the music fans of America, are distinguished Ponca singers who have widely traveled, recorded their tribal songs, and are well known in American Indian music circles. This group has performed in Florida, California, and most states of the West and Midwest and are constantly in demand to provide the musical background wherever Indians congregate to relive the good old days. Indeed, the Indians themselves have placed a special value on the old-time songs so well sung by the Ponca, as opposed to some of the newer songs which travel the powwow circuit each year.

One Ponca should be noted in particular. His name is Clyde Warrior, and before his untimely death at the age of twenty-nine, he was one of the most vociferous leaders of the National Indian Youth Council, an organization formed to fight for the equality of the American Indian. Clyde led one of the first Indian demonstrations—a fish-in in the state of Washington—after local Indians were denied their right to fish certain areas guaranteed them by treaty. Warrior died of the white man's legacy—

alcoholism—and was buried by his grandfather on Indian land in White Eagle, Oklahoma, the town named after another great Ponca chief.

The Quapaw

Another tribe of the five Dhegiha-speaking Siouans who migrated from the Southeast to the Prairies by way of the Great Lakes was the Quapaw (sometimes spelled Kwapa). Their name comes from *Ugakhpa*, meaning "downstream people," to distinguish them from the "Omaha," or "upstream people." The latter settled on the Missouri River, while the Quapaw moved south to the Arkansas River in the present state of Arkansas.

The Quapaw were a peaceful, agricultural people who lived in three fortified villages. Their homes were long bark houses with dome-shaped roofs built on mounds of earth. In addition to cultivating corn, squash, beans, and pumpkins, the Quapaw were fine pottery makers.

The Spaniards, the first whites to meet the Quapaw in 1541, reported their numbers at five to six thousand. This seems an excessive figure, for in 1829 there were only 500 Quapaw. In a treaty of 1818, the Quapaw ceded all their lands in Arkansas and moved to Louisiana. Disliking the area, they pleaded with the government to let them return to their original home. Finally, in 1833, they were relocated in Indian Territory. Some members scattered and took up residence with other tribes already established in Oklahoma.

During the Civil War the Quapaw served with the Union Army. After the war some returned to their reservation in Indian Territory while others moved in with other tribes. Not until 1887, the year of the Indian Allotment Act in which each Indian was allotted a specific number of acres for his individual ownership and use (as opposed to communal ownership of reservation land), did the Quapaw return to their agency. But, unhappy with the terms of the allotment in which each head of household received only 80 acres, though there was enough reservation land to entitle each family a larger estate, the Quapaw set a precedent for all tribes by taking the matter of allotting land into their own hands. With the help of whites who were paid and given full membership in the Quapaw tribe, the tribal leaders won legal battles that gave 200 acres to each member—including the whites who aided them. Thus today, the Quapaw tribal rolls list a number of full-blooded white Quapaws.

In 1905 lead and zinc were found on the Quapaw land, which brought in royalties of more than $1,500,-000 a year. The royalties were used by the Quapaw to improve their land, build schools, and develop a number of other civic enterprises which were shared with the whites who lived around them.

Today, the Quapaw number something over 1,000 and live in Ottawa County, Oklahoma, near the town of Miami.

The Tonkawa

Although cannibalism was relatively unknown in the United States, the Tonkawa are said to have practiced it in ancient times. Actually there is little to corroborate the report, other than occasional mention of the Tonkawa "cooking a young Caddo in preparation of a feast," and the fact that the Kiowa and Comanche referred to the Tonkawa as man-eating men.

The Tonkawa were originally composed of a number of small tribes which roved across central Texas, western Oklahoma, and eastern New Mexico where they were hostile to the Lipan Apache. They lived in tepees, were considered excellent horsemen, and hunted buffalo and deer for their livelihood. They were the only representatives of the Tonkawan linguistic family. The word "Tonkawa" comes from the Waco term meaning "they all stay together."

The Tonkawa were reported to have been extremely warlike, fighting the Apache, Spanish, and Americans. They were originally friendly with the Comanche and Caddoan tribes until some Tonkawa joined the U.S. Army as scouts in campaigns against these tribes, thus alienating them. In 1862, some Delaware, Shawnee, Wichita, and Caddo attacked the Tonkawa, massacring 167 men, women, and children. Only those Tonkawa who had been away on a buffalo hunt survived. Their population, estimated at 1,500 in 1778, became almost extinct. Only 46 were alive in 1936.

During the Civil War the Tonkawa served with the Confederate Army and were eventually allotted land in Indian Territory, in what is now Kay County, Oklahoma, near the town of Tonkawa. Their population is currently fewer than 100 persons.

The Wichita

The Wichita, members of the Caddoan linguistic family and closely related to the Pawnee, were originally a confederacy composed of the Wichita proper, Tawakoni, Waco, and Kichai. The tribal name comes from the Choctaw *wia chitoh*, meaning "big arbor," describing the large grass houses with dome roofs which were the traditional dwellings of the Wichita. The Wichita called themselves *Kitikitish*, meaning "raccoon-eyed," referring to their method of face painting and tattooing in ancient times. The Kiowa and Comanche also called them tattooed people while the Caddo called them *tawehash*, or "traders." They are also listed under a variety of names in historical accounts: The Spanish called them *Jumano*, a corruption of an Indian word meaning "drummers"; the Siouans called them *Paniwasaba*, or "black Pawnee"; and because of their relation to the Pawnee tribe and tradition of tattooing, the French called them *Pani Pique*.

The original Wichita confederacy lived on the Arkansas River in Oklahoma and the Red and Brazos rivers in Texas. They were agriculturists, raising corn, squash, melons, pumpkins, and tobacco, and they were also hunters. They fought the Apache, Comanche, and Osage. Their population was estimated at 3,200 in 1778, and 2,000 in 1805.

In 1858, while the Comanche were visiting a Wichita village, they were attacked by U.S. troops who destroyed the village, crops, and possessions in a fierce fight known as the Battle of Wichita Village. Ironically, Captain Earl Van Dorn, of the Second United States Calvary, who was bent on destroying the "wild Comanches," was unaware that the Comanche had just returned from a peace conference with the federal government. Though the Wichita were involved only by a stroke of misfortune, the Comanche from that period on suspected them of conspiring with federal troops in arranging the attack.

During the Civil War some of the Wichita sided with the Confederacy, others with the Union. Those who fought with the South were unhappy with the terms of the treaty and soon moved to Kansas, near the city which today bears their name. In 1867 the Wichita were settled in Indian Territory in Caddo country near the town of Gracemont, where they now live. Because of epidemics, their numbers were reduced to 153 in 1894. Today they are counted with the Tawakoni, Waco, Kichai, and Hanai, and number approximately 400.

Pawnee earth lodge village located on the Loup Fork. Taken by William H. Jackson in 1871. (*Smithsonian Institution*)

3

Hunters and Farmers

BEFORE THE age of industrialization man was faced with obtaining food, clothing, shelter, transportation, from nature itself. Man's development of his economy and sustenance has been inescapably bound to his environment. The kinds of animals and plant life that existed around him determined his diet and kind of clothing. Climate, topography, the quantity of wood, water, and animal life, determined the nature of his housing, transportation, and social organization. His very survival depended on his ability to understand Mother Earth.

Indians who found all that was necessary to sustain life in their immediate vicinity usually lived in permanent or semipermanent villages. Those who had to search constantly for food became nomadic. Because of drought, famine, or aggression by hostile tribes, many tribes were forced to change their environment. In doing so, they learned to conform to the new lands into which they moved.

Most of the principal Southern Plains tribes originally lived in permanent or semipermanent villages and were primarily agriculturists, sometimes augmenting their vegetable diets with meat which they hunted away from their villages. This was especially true of two large groups: the Siouan-speaking Omaha, Osage, Ponca, Kansa, Quapaw, Iowa, and Oto-Missouri; and the Caddoan-speaking Pawnee and Wichita, with their various subtribes and bands.

All these tribes migrated from the Southeast, bringing with them a rich cultural heritage from their original homeland. They continued their agricultural way of life. Most of the tribes moved to regions surrounded by lakes, and later, along large rivers where adjacent lands were rich and easily cultivated. There they built villages and cultivated gardens which yielded the traditional indigenous crops of the United States: corn, squash, beans, pumpkins, melons, tobacco.

Some gardens were small; others were real farms. The Indians developed utensils they needed for the planting and harvesting of crops: hoes, rakes, digging sticks for planting seeds, and packs and baskets for collecting and storing their food. They knew how to rotate their crops to wrest the maximum food from the earth. They used fertilizers and prepared their fields for the planting of new crops by a technique called slash and burn. The ground was plowed and slashed, and then a wood fire was built on top so that ashes would restore the soil. The Indians augmented their diet by collecting a multitude of wild berries, nuts, and vegetables. There was some fishing, and fowl was hunted with bow and arrow.

The predominant type of house of the agriculturists was originally the earth lodge. Each lodge was built to accommodate several related families. Some large villages contained as many as two hundred of these lodges, and many of the villages were fortified with surrounding palisades for protection against hostile tribes. The lodges were arbitrarily arranged in the village, allowing for some cleared places where religious ceremonies were held. Often the village was dominated by a larger earth lodge which was used for ceremonies during cold or inclement weather.

The usual earth lodge measured 30 to 40 feet in diameter, 10 to 15 feet in height at the center, and 5 to 7 feet at the eaves. Lodges were constructed by both men and women. First the floor was dug out of the earth to a depth of about 1 foot, then tamped down to form a solid base. Logs from the riverbanks served as uprights, which were placed around the circumference of the lodge exterior. Four posts were erected in the center and joined together by beams.

Rafters were laid from the center beams to the outside uprights. Smaller saplings were woven into the superstructure and covered with brush and grass. The entire framework was then covered with earth so that none of the superstructure was visible from the outside. The entrance was tunnel-like and also made from logs covered with brush and earth. It could be closed off in winter with doors made of mats and hides. The roofs of the lodges were used to dry foods and were strong enough to support many people who might want to sit on top and watch ceremonial events.

Inside the earth lodge, small compartments for sleeping and storing one's personal belongings were arranged around the inside wall. The beds and seating benches were made from saplings, woven mats, and animal skins. The compartments could be partitioned off with skin drapes for privacy. Cooking was communally done by the several families residing in the earth lodge. Smoke from the fire escaped from a hole in the top of the roof, which also allowed light to enter the lodge. In some lodges there was even a palisaded section to keep horses at night, lest they be stolen by hostile tribes.

But the Caddoan and Siouan peoples were only *primarily* agriculturists. They had come to their new homes on the rugged plains and prairies in search of that magnificent creature whose herds darkened the prairies for miles upon miles—the buffalo.

Of all sources of life for the Plains Indian, the buffalo was most important. Literally hundreds of uses were derived from the shaggy beast's hide, meat, bone, and horn. It provided warm robes, clothing, coverings for tepees, cooking and eating utensils, domestic raw materials for making weapons and articles of religious import. Its meat was a basic diet. Buffalo was so important that it was often elevated to the role of a deity, and many ceremonies and dances were performed in its honor to secure good luck on the hunt. It had been placed on the earth, the Indians said, to provide all the necessities of life.

In early days, before the horse, the buffalo was hunted on foot with bow and arrow or spears. Buffalo runs—long lines of warriors waving robes to frighten the animal—could be used to stampede herds over cliffs where they fell to death. Women would stand at the bottom of the cliff and club or spear animals which had only been wounded by the fall. The buffalo then was skinned on the spot and hides and meat carried by dog travois—a V-shaped drag—back to the village.

Of equal importance to the Plains Indian was the horse. Probably no single phenomenon so changed the living pattern of the Indian. Hunters and warriors who once made long treks on foot across the Plains in search of game or war now were mobilized. On horseback they had the speed of the buffalo and no longer had to resort to falls, snares, traps, and decoys. Armed with bow and arrow or lance, they could ride right into the herd, carefully select a fat bull or cow, and kill the animal. The

Buffalo skin on drying rack, Indian City, U. S. A., Anadarko, Oklahoma. (*Marla Powers*)

buffalo chase also added adventure to an already hazardous way of life; if the Indian pony should slip, the hunter might be trampled to death by the massive beasts. The horse also made it easier to transport heavier loads and move quickly against one's enemy. Horse stealing became a favorite pastime of the Plains Indian. One's wealth was determined by the number of horses he owned; horses brought prestige.

It has been estimated by most experts that the Indians of the Southern Plains began to obtain horses around 1600. Probably the first to receive them were the Apache, Comanche, Kiowa, and Caddo. The horse had been introduced by the Spanish, who taught their Indian slaves how to ride and tend their horses. The most acceptable theory is that the Indian slaves in turn taught other Indians how to ride as well as make all the equipment needed for riding and maintenance of the horse. For example, the typical Indian saddle, with a high seat and pommel, resembles the old Spanish saddles. Most Indians were equally at ease riding bareback and guiding the horse with knees or a braided rope. The Indians became so proficient with the horse that "to ride like a Comanche" was a compliment to both Indian and white on the Southern Plains. Many Indians and whites who faced the Comanche agreed that he was unequaled as a cavalryman.

By 1725 almost all tribes of the Southern Plains were mounted. The horse enabled them to make long forays against other tribes as well as the Mexicans, who for many years lived in constant fear of the Apache and Comanche. Not only the nomadic Apache, Comanche, and Kiowa relied on the horse and buffalo for obtaining food, clothing, shelter, and a life of war. The agriculturists also hunted buffalo on horseback, leaving their fortified villages and packing small tepees which they had learned to make to provide shelter during their hunting trips. Like the nomads, the agriculturists also used the hides of the buffalo for their dwellings and clothing. In addition to hunting, many agriculturists traded their crops in exchange for hides and furs from the more nomadic peoples who devoted most of their time to wresting a living from the rolling plains. Over a short period the Caddoan and Siouan peoples became full-fledged Plains and Prairie dwelling people. While still maintaining their gardens, they entered into the thrill and adventure of the buffalo chase.

The Cheyenne and Arapaho had originally come from the Southeast, following the route of the Siouan speakers to the Great Lakes. But they forgot they too once had lived in agricultural villages in Minnesota, after they became tepee-dwelling nomads of the Plains. They shared with other Northern tribes, such as the Kiowa and Kiowa Apache who migrated southward, a tepee built on a three-poled base and lashed at the top of the tripod. The agriculturists followed this method of making their tepees. The Comanche, however, used a four-poled base for their tepees, which they also lashed at the top. This made the Comanche tepee unique, for traditionally all four-pole-based-tepee users did not find it necessary to lash the base together. Additional poles were added to both types, and a circular covering of buffalo hides was placed over the framework to form the shelter. The tepee was easily dismantled when a tribe moved out to hunt and easily assembled when it came together again for councils and religious meetings.

The tepee dwellers came together in a predetermined pattern. Each half tribe took its respective side of the camp circle. The Ponca camped in three concentric circles, while the Omaha camped in two, thus causing

the Sioux to nickname them the Three Tribes and Two
Tribes, respectively. When not camped in the tribal
circle, the bands usually set up their camps in any manner convenient to them, taking into consideration the
natural windbreaks of hills and wooded ravines in the

Tepee village and brush arbors at Indian City, U. S. A. (*Marla Powers*)

winter. Usually each tepee housed only one family, though related persons might pitch their tepees near one another.

Inside the tepee a central fireplace provided warmth and cooking space in the winter. Cooking was usually done outdoors in the summer, either in the open air or in special cook shades made from willow saplings. Beds and seats made from willow reeds tied together were placed around the inside circumference of the tepee and covered with hides and furs. The smoke from the fire escaped through the smoke hole, which could be regulated by moving the ears of the tepee, located at the top where the poles were lashed together. The ears could be opened or closed depending on the weather. Often an inner lining of skin, called a dew cloth, was hung inside the tepee from the poles for extra insulation. In very cold weather the Indians often built a brush wind-break around the exterior.

The tepee could be moved from one hunting ground to another by horseback. Usually two or three horses were needed, one pulling a travois, made from two tepee poles, which bore personal belongings or children and the very old. The other horses carried the hide cover and the rest of the tepee poles. In crossing streams the entire travois could be floated to the opposite bank. The travois was originally attached to the shoulders of dogs by straps before the advent of the horse. After the Indians received horses, the tepees were much larger owing to the horses' ability to pull larger loads.

One peculiar type of dwelling imported from the Southeast and used widely by the Caddoan-speaking tribes was a lodge covered with grass, popularly known as the Wichita grass house.

The dwelling had a circular base of saplings which were joined at the top with thongs giving the effect of a

Wichita Indians build a grass house at the Omaha Exposition in 1898. (*Smithsonian Institution*)

A Wichita camp showing a grass house, an open-sided shelter, and a tepee frame. The photographer and date are not recorded. (*Smithsonian Institution*)

Gothic dome. Similarly, smaller saplings were horizontally placed around the circumference and lashed to the uprights. The entire framework was then covered with bundles of grass to produce a shingled effect. The average dwelling was fifteen feet high, with one doorway. Larger council houses were two or three times larger and had four doorways. Platforms for sleeping were placed around the inner circumference of the house, and there was a single cooking fire in the center which was shared by a number of families. Because of the size and structure, no smoke hole was needed. Often a shade was erected next to the grass house. It was generally elliptical at the base and the roof was more oval than dome. The walls were left open to allow cool breezes to blow through in hot summers.

Though the Apache were tepee dwellers, they also constructed a small dwelling called a wickiup. The wickiup might be a simple dome-shaped structure built

Apache wickiup at Indian City, U. S. A., Anadarko, Oklahoma. (*Marla Powers*)

from saplings tied together to form framework and covered with brush and skins. Others were more elaborate, having a side entrance which led into a two-level domed house about 6 feet high. The grass thatching and skins were held in place by saplings bent around the circumference of the structure and lashed together. As in the other dwellings, beds were placed around the inner walls of the house and there was a central cooking fire. The wickiup was large enough to accommodate one family.

Arbors were used by many of the tribes for cooking or sleeping during the summer when it was very hot. Most were oval-shaped and constructed of saplings covered with willow branches.

Sweat lodges were constructed for health and religious purposes. The small dome-shaped buildings were for purification by steam, much like the modern sauna. A hole was dug in the center of the lodge and white-hot stones placed in the hole. The framework was then covered with mats and hides to make it airtight, and cool water was sprinkled over the stones to create steam.

After European traders reached the Indians, they brought many things which changed the Indians' way of living. Skin tents were soon replaced by canvas. Canvas was light but durable and enabled the tepee dwellers to build even larger homes. Four-walled tents were commercially manufactured for the Indians' use, and slowly but surely the square tent replaced the traditional tepee. Many Indians today, though living in frame houses, own tents which they set up at Indian gatherings. A few still own tepees, mainly for religious rites.

The white man also brought new methods of transportation. The travois fell into disuse after the introduction of the wagon, which was used to move tepees as well as four-walled tents.

Osage Indian dancers line up in front of a typical dance lodge at

Gray Horse, Oklahoma, around 1912. (*Smithsonian Institution*)

With the exception of a few archaic homes, such as the earth lodge and grass house which are preserved in a museumlike atmosphere in Indian City, U.S.A., near Anadarko, Oklahoma, all vestiges of the old dwellings have disappeared. Today the Southern Plains Indians live in small communities scattered across Oklahoma and parts of Kansas and Nebraska in homes indistinguishable from those of their non-Indian neighbors. Only during fair time, or at many of the small tribal powwows, do the Indians live in tents and tepees.

At the fairs and powwows the camps are crowded with members of many tribes who camp out in tents and tepees and build willow cook shades and sunshades close to their shelters. Often the Indians bring along spring mattress beds and other conveniences from their homes. The automobile has to some degree changed the appearance of the once overcrowded camps, since some Indians now prefer to commute from their homes to the campgrounds. But many of the old-timers still prefer to stay all night at the grounds where they can listen to the drumming and singing until they drift off to sleep.

While most of the powwows and fairs are held outdoors, there was one special kind of dance hall used by the Osage and Pawnee which resembled a wooden version of an earth lodge. Traditionally called a dance house and made of planked walls and ceiling, with a dirt floor, the house was used for meetings and dances. It was multisided. Some had a roof, others were open at the top but enclosed at the eaves. In the center of the dance house, benches were arranged in a circle for the singers. Other benches were built along the inside circumference of the wall to accommodate dancers and spectators.

The most popular dance arena today is the shade, or dance arbor. It is usually circular or semicircular and is constructed of two concentric circles of uprights which are joined and covered over with brush to form a sunshade for spectators. The central area where the dancing takes place is open. Benches are arranged under the shade for the exclusive use of the dancers who wish to rest between dances.

The automobile has become as indispensable to the Indian as his horse was in days past. The Southern Plains tribes located in Oklahoma travel frequently to other communities in the state and go great distances to other reservations to participate in tribal events, such as powwows, fairs, and rodeos. Because of easy accessibility, cities like Tulsa and Oklahoma City have become the centers of many intertribal events. The great rutted trails created by the poles of the old-time travois have been replaced by modern turnpikes and the famous Route 66, which bisects the state of Oklahoma east and west. Other modern highways take you quickly to the small towns north and south where the small, scattered Indian communities are located. Despite their integration into predominantly white communities, the Indians of the Southern Plains hold fast to their traditions. During the summer months the highways are filled with autos carrying a still-nomadic people to places where drums throb and the high-pitched voices of singers call the dancers to assemble. Dwellings and methods of transportation have changed drastically, but the Indian spirit remains immutable.

Burial scaffold at Indian City, U. S. A. (*Marla Powers*)

4

The Life Cycle

No TWO events in the life cycle of the American Indian were more heralded or bemoaned than birth and death. The newborn replenished the population of the tribe, thus offering security to its members in terms of future warriors and mothers. Those who died in battle or of old age went to live for eternity in a spirit world.

These two significant aspects of the life cycle have always been foremost in the thinking of the American Indian. Every society has its special ceremonies to welcome the newborn and lament the departed. The American Indian is no exception. Stepping stones of the life cycle through its many stages from infancy to old age were likewise celebrated by elaborate ritual marked by mysterious taboos. The child was educated to take his role in the society and become a productive member. His education was largely through careful instruction by his elders, imitation of their life-style, and games of skill and chance which eventually taught him the strategy he needed to fulfill his obligations to the tribe. The rites of passage, as they are sometimes called, the movement from one stage of life to another, were each celebrated with speeches, music, dance, and the bestowal of special names and honors upon the subject. Ceremonies differed from tribe to tribe, but the significance of attaining a new place in one's life was of universal importance.

Birth was both a wondrous and mysterious occasion. When the time came for the birth of the child, the expectant mother was moved to a special hut where she was accompanied by a midwife—an older woman who herself had experienced childbirth. It was taboo for the men to approach the hut; male doctors did not attend such matters. When the child was born, his umbilical cord was cut and tied. The cord itself was placed in an elaborately designed pouch, often in the form of a turtle or other animal, and attached to the newborn as a good luck charm. The charm might be worn for several years before the mother carefully stored it away as a memento.

An infant spent most of his time in a cradleboard which could be carried on his mother's back, leaned against the lodge while his mother worked, or suspended from a tree or tripod where the gentle winds rocked the baby to sleep. The cradleboard was often constructed with a face guard of wood circumscribing the child's head; if the cradleboard should accidentally fall, his face would be protected.

Announcement of a birth was usually heralded by the camp crier, who informed the village of the sex of the child and when he would be named. The naming ceremony itself was elaborate and accompanied by gift giving among the relatives of the child. The name might signify an important event that had happened when the child was born, or the infant might be named after a deceased member of the tribe. Often the child's name would be frequently changed as he achieved new status. Among the Iowa, a man might have as many as six or seven names during a lifetime. Many Indians had both a given name and a nickname, much as young non-Indian children do.

The child's education was largely a matter of imitating the skills and roles of his mother and father. Young girls played with dolls, constructed miniature tepees and clothing, and eventually learned to cook, make clothing, and construct the ever-important tepee. Boys were given small bows and arrows and encouraged to hunt small birds or participate in games of skill. These included target shooting; war games; hoop and javelin, in which opposing teams tried to spear a rolling hoop; snow snake, a competition in which wooden snakes were thrown down a runway of ice to see whose snake traveled farthest. As boys grew older they were charged with the responsibility of guarding the horses. They became expert horsemen at an early age and much of their time was spent in learning the art of hunting on horseback. Their horsemanship was developed by horse races, a favorite leisure pastime.

In addition to games of skill and strategy, there were many games of chance. Often they were accompanied by heavy gambling. The most popular games of chance, played by both men and women, were the dice game and a form of guessing game, sometimes called moccasin game. Dice were made from cherry and plum stones or small bits of bone painted or etched to indicate their value. The dice were usually tossed from a wooden bowl or basket and the way in which they landed on a blanket indicated the score. In the guessing game an object such as a small rock was hidden beneath one of two or more bowls or moccasins, and the opponent had to guess correctly under which cover the rock was hidden. Often these games were accompanied by rapid drumming and singing to help confuse the guesser. Scores were kept by means of tally sticks. Often entire clans might challenge one another to the game.

Among the Kansa the guessing game was played with a small bullet hidden in one hand, in which the first and second fingers were outstretched. While the guesser tried to decide in which hand the bullet was hidden, the opponent switched it back and forth from one hand to the other behind his back. If the person guessing was correct, he was entitled to hide the bullet. The Kansa women used a bell in the moccasin game. Four moccasins were used and the bell hidden under one of them. In the women's version of the game, a small girl held a buffalo robe over the moccasins while the bell was being hidden. The Kansa men called the game *humbeblaska*, or "flat moccasin."

In the Kansa form of the dice game there were eight dice made from filed-down brass tacks obtained from traders. Two tacks were painted red and blue on one side; the others were unpainted. The dice were tossed from a wooden bowl, and the way the painted dice fell determined the score. The game was called *kansiku*.

By the time a young boy reached the age of eleven or twelve he might be invited to accompany a war party. At that age the boy did not fight, but performed chores for the warriors, such as gathering firewood and water or carrying extra supplies. He was also encouraged to accompany the men on the buffalo hunts, and his first kill was highly acclaimed by his family and other members of the tribe. At that age he also was taught the traditional lore of his tribe—the stories, history, and religion. He soon learned the importance of religious training and was trained in the proper respect for the

pipe, medicine bundles, and other religious paraphernalia of the tribe. Young people were admonished if
they did not behave properly during religious convocations or if they touched sacred objects which were the
strict domain of the medicine men and shamans. Only
after a boy had reached maturity could he participate in
the sacred ceremonies of the tribe.

One of the most important times in the young boy's
life was when he was ready to make the vision quest.
After consultation with a shaman, the boy would be
placed on a hill away from camp. Alone he would stay
on top of the hill, fasting and praying until he received
a vision. In the dream he might be visited by animals or
inanimate objects which would talk to him, or possibly
teach him sacred songs. The boy, upon returning to the
village, would seek out the shaman to interpret the
dream. If the boy was visited by an animal, the shaman
might require him to hunt the animal and to use a portion of the animal as a good luck charm for hunting or
in battle. Often the young boy was warned never to eat
the meat of the animal which served as his charm.
Sometimes the charms were worn on one's person, or
they were kept in his medicine bundle, which was
opened only on special occasions when the power of the
spirit was invoked.

When a young man had proved himself successful in
hunting and warfare and had been asked to join one of
the numerous men's societies, he was then eligible to
take a bride. Among the Southern Plains tribes girls
usually married in their midteens, men in their late
teens or early twenties. Some tribes practiced polygamy,
but a man had to be prosperous in order to support
more than one wife. So the practice was not as widespread as one might suppose.

Courtship was no easy matter because the young

maiden was always chaperoned by her grandmother or another older female relative. Rarely was she left alone, except when attending to some daily tasks such as gathering firewood or water. Her suitor would wait for such moments as these when he could meet his sweetheart along a path that led to a stream. When she passed, he would call her name or tug at her garment. If she liked him, she would stop and talk and possibly arrange another rendezvous. If she did not, she would pass by quickly—much to the dismay of the jilted suitor.

A favorite way of getting the attention of the girl was to play a love flute outside her lodge door, usually from a place of seclusion. The girl could recognize the flute melody and know her suitor was near. Other courtships were more formal. At certain times of the evening the girl would be allowed to step outside her lodge door and see one or several suitors who lined up to speak to her about the possibilities of marriage. The custom among the Ponca and other Siouan tribes was for the boy and girl to stand close with his blanket drawn over her shoulder. There they would talk until either the girl had heard enough of the proposal or a competitive suitor called that time was up, and the next in line took his turn. The young men wore special courting blankets, usually made from dark-blue trade cloth decorated with a single, beaded band down the center.

While the marriage ceremony itself was very often simply an exchange of gifts between the parents of the bride and bridegroom and the establishment of a new home for the married couple, there were other factors which governed the eligibility of married people. A man could not arbitrarily marry the woman of his choice. The women available to him were predetermined by the tribal system of marriage practice.

Since it offers clues as to why certain people react in

An Omaha Indian, Ni-ka-ga-hi, wearing a yarn-woven turban, plays a love flute. Photographed by Alice C. Fletcher in 1911. (*Smithsonian Institution*)

the way they do to others in their society, let us consider something that many anthropologists consider the most important in investigating a group of people. The subject is called kinship systems.

Kinship is not only one of the most important studies of human behavior, but one of the most difficult. In our own society we take for granted the names we use to refer to the members of our family—mother, father, sister, brother, and the like. We also take for granted that a newly married couple will eventually live in their own home, which they will establish independently from their parents. In the larger study of kinship we not only investigate kinship terminology (how people address each other in terms of relationship) but also lineage (whether or not we claim a common ancestor) and residence (where we reside after marriage). There are a number of technical terms used to describe all facets of kinship. These terms at times become outmoded and are replaced by new ones. Some terms duplicate themselves, hence a mild confusion sets in on one who begins to study kinship. But since kinship predetermines how people in any given society behave toward one another, a simplified introduction seems relevant in discussing Indians of the Southern Plains.

First of all, there are three kinds of relationship: consanguineal, or actual blood relationship such as between a mother and son, brother and sister, and the like; affinal, which is relationship through marriage, such as husband and wife, and their respective in-laws; and fictive (compare the word with "fictitious"), accomplished through the act of adopting someone. In our own system we can readily identify who are our blood relatives, relatives by marriage, and foster children. But in most Indian societies the terms used to identify kin are different from ours. Among some tribes a man may actually have four mothers, three fathers, and the people whom we normally call cousin may in fact be called brother and sister. Among other groups of people, every kinship term is a descriptive term. In other words, instead of calling a man grandfather, he would be referred to as my father's father, or mother's father.

There are only six systems of kinship in the world, plus some variations. Four of them are named after American Indian tribes—Omaha, Crow, Iroquoian, and Eskimo. The Euro-American system which we use in this country is strangely enough the Eskimo system. That is to say, the Eskimo use the same kinship terms we do. The other two systems are the Hawaiian and Sudanese.

In our own system it is clear whom we can or cannot marry. Legally, as well as morally, for instance, marriage between brother and sister, first cousins, or essentially blood relatives is prohibited. The same is true among Indian tribes. However, according to what system is followed, the Indian may consider those people we call distant relatives as blood relatives. Consequently, some marriages sanctioned by our system would not be sanctioned by Indians.

In addition to marriage rights, kinship also operates as a regulator for inheritance. Usually, blood relatives are considered the rightful heirs to money, real estate, and other property. The same is true in Indian society, but again those considered blood relatives may well go beyond our concepts. Thus learning about the kinship terms used by any given tribe tells us a great deal about their behavior and traditions.

Some Americans take great pride in tracing their ancestry back to the Pilgrims or royal families of Europe. Phrasing it in kinship terminology, they enjoy tracing their line of descent. Indians, too, are specific about tracing their common ancestry, only in their case the common ancestor may be a real person or a mythical being. Families that shared a common ancestor, real or mythical, formed clans within a tribe. If the common ancestor was traced through the father, the lineage system is called patrilineal; if through the mother's side, matrilineal. Some tribes believed that it was wrong to marry within one's own clan (that is, they could only marry someone from another clan) and practiced exogamy (to marry out). Some believed that their clan could only be strengthened by retaining as many members as possible; therefore, people were required to marry within the clan, a practice called endogamy (to marry in). Even though a woman takes a man's family name in marriage in our society, both husband and wife claim their line of descent, a practice called ambilineality (both lines). And, of course, legally one man can be married to only one woman at one time, a practice called monogamy (to marry one). The Pawnee were endogamous, while the Ponca and other Siouan speakers were exogamous.

We have seen that tribes such as the Iowa, Omaha, and Ponca were divided into half tribes, and in turn each half tribe contained a number of smaller groups called clans. The technical term for a half tribe is "moiety" (from the French word for "half a society"). This indicated that *where* people lived after marriage —that is, the place of their new residence—was also an important factor in the study of American Indian tribes. Among some tribes, the newly married couple moved in with the husband's people. This is called patrilocal residence. The reverse is matrilocal residence. If the couple moved to a home independent of either's family, it is called neolocal (new place). Most

Indians living today on the Southern Plains are neo-local, mostly due to white influence and intertribal marriages.

To illustrate the mechanics of kinship, let's examine one of the six systems named after a Southern Plains tribe, the Omaha. The Omaha system is typical of the Siouan-speaking tribes. The Omaha were divided into two half tribes, or moieties. Each moiety was made up of a number of clans. The members of the clans traced their ancestry through the male side of the family, thus were patrilineal. Upon marriage, a man and his wife usually moved into the lodge of his father. Often, during the earth lodge period, several brothers and their wives occupied the same lodge, hence were patrilocal. One thing that will seem unusual to us who are concerned with generations is that in the Omaha system, generations were sometimes skipped. Thus it was possible, according to the Omaha system, to have an uncle who was younger than you and a grandchild who was older! Although this arrangement seems strange to those accustomed to relating kinship by generation, it proves that the study of kinship itself is extremely important in order to fully understand any group of people. Undoubtedly the Omaha of yesteryear would find our system (and the Eskimo's) difficult to understand too.

In our own society we joke about our relatives—especially mothers-in-law. The Indians, too, had a number of joking relationships, as well as kinship taboos. The most widespread joking relationship was that between brothers-in-law. Custom dictated that whenever two brothers-in-law met, they had to joke with each other, often in a derogatory manner. They often degraded each other's hunting, war achievements, the manner in which they dressed or ate, and the frequency with which they chased women. Because the joking was required conduct, hostilities never arose between the brothers-in-law, no matter how low the blows. I have heard brothers-in-law degrade and make fun of each other for hours upon end, much to the amusement of other relatives who listen with glee. Often two or more brothers will gang up on a single brother-in-law, each trying to top the other's joke. Listening to this kind of conversation, one certainly rejects the theory that Indians are stoic.

The most common kinship taboo was mother-in-law avoidance. Men were not allowed to speak to or even look at their mothers-in-law. The same rule held true in many instances with a woman and her father-in-law. If a man saw his mother-in-law approaching, he might take great pains to go out of his way to avoid her. Most Indians claim that the avoidance taboo was adhered to out of respect to the wife's mother. The practice is still observed by many Indians today, though not as strongly as in the past.

A person who reached old age, as long as he could function, usually fulfilled the role of councilman or adviser. Thus among such tribes as the Cheyenne and Arapaho, the tribal leaders were usually older men whose life experience guided the actions of their tribesmen. The elders who could no longer hunt or fight were provided for by the younger people of the village.

It has been noted among many Indian tribes, especially the more nomadic such as the Kiowa and Comanche, that persons reaching old age sometimes elected to commit suicide or separate themselves from the traveling band to remain alone in a tepee until they died of starvation. In some rare instances the old might be killed because they could no longer provide for themselves and became a burden to a society that was constantly on the move in search of food. It should be emphasized that murder of the aged or infirm was rare. Most elderly people elected to remain in isolation, usually in a tepee with a minimal amount of food, until the food ran out and they died. While the practice of abandoning the old seems inhumane, there were reasons other than the burden they presented to fellow members of the tribe. Some, for instance, believed that an older person was more vulnerable to evil spirits and his very presence might bring calamity to the village.

There were several forms of rituals of the dead and burial customs among the Southern Plains tribes. Among the Comanche, for example, the deceased was usually placed in a sitting position with his knees folded against his chest and his head bent forward. The limbs were secured with bindings and the body placed in a blanket where it remained in state for a short period. The body was then transported to a burial place by horseback. The ideal site was a natural cave or crevice where the body was placed in a sitting position. Food, clothing, and weapons were interred with the body so that the deceased might have all he required for his extended spirit life in another world.

Most of the Siouan speakers, the Omaha, Osage, Ponca, Quapaw, Kansa, Oto-Missouri, and Iowa, originally buried their dead in shallow graves which were covered with earth and stones. Among the Caddo, Wichita, and Pawnee, the graves often resembled small earth lodges which were arranged in a group in a village cemetery. Often a pen or stockade was built around each grave to prevent wild animals from devouring the bodies.

Some tribes practiced more than one form of burial, the nature of which was largely determined by the terrain. A common type among the Cheyenne, Arapaho, Comanche, Kiowa, Kiowa Apache, and later the Siouan speakers was the tree or scaffold burial. The body was dressed in fine clothes, the face painted, and then wrapped in a buffalo hide which was placed high in the crotch of a tree. If in a treeless area, the tribes often erected a burial scaffold atop four uprights onto which the body was placed. Often a favorite horse was killed and placed beneath the scaffold so that the deceased might have it to ride on his journey to the spirit world.

The period of mourning often lasted as long as a year. Close relatives would paint their faces black, cut their hair short, or otherwise scarify their arms and legs to show their bereavement. Often the relative would moan and wail near the grave, even though there was a common belief that such places abounded with spirits. Rarely was a grave molested by hostile tribes because of the fear of retribution by the spirits—if not during this lifetime, during the next.

In some unusual cases a warrior killed in battle might not be buried at all but left for wild animals to devour. It was believed by a few that the warrior's power would then be cast all over the area in which his tribe lived and would serve to protect them.

The land of the departed spirits, though not always clearly defined, seemed to be similar to the earthly world. The Omaha, as one example, envisioned the hereafter as a village of brave and generous souls which they called *Wanagoti*, or "village of ghosts." Entrance into this hereafter was based on a person's generosity and goodwill during life. If he lived a good life and provided for his people, he would eventually go to *Wanagoti*. If not, he would reside permanently in a spirit village made up of poor and decadent people.

Many Indians believed that the spirit of the deceased was capable of reappearing on earth and visiting with relatives. Often these spirits were called upon by religious practitioners to reveal powers of curing.

Thus to the Indian people the life cycle was never-ending. The spirit lived on to greet the spirits of friends and relatives who died later, resuming the earthly way of life—hunting, planting, and even warring against the spirits of hostile tribes.

A gathering of Kiowa Indians at the Lawton, Oklahoma, arena in 1970. Gourd dancers are at right.

5

Military and Social Organizations

MOTION PICTURES and television have gone to great lengths to disgrace and stereotype the American Indian, especially regarding the subject of warfare. One becomes bored with the oft-repeated scenes of Indians attacking wagon trains, burning forts, and torturing victims. Flaming arrows and bloodcurdling screams reign supreme; the blond scalp of a pioneer woman flies triumphantly from the warrior's lodge. Few people realize that it was the white man who taught the Indian the practice of scalping, that in all probability more Indians were scalped than whites—and not necessarily by other Indians.

If we remove ourselves from the constricted portrait of the bloodthirsty renegade stalking helpless settlers, we are often thrown to the other side of the Indian stereotype. This includes the noble, altruistic Hiawatha of Longfellow's creation; the loyal, self-sacrificing Uncas and Chingachagook of James Fenimore Cooper's *Leatherstocking Tales*; and the ultimate in the white man's concept of the Indian—Tonto, the masked man's faithful companion who, judging by the number of speaking lines he is given in any Lone Ranger movie, has an intelligence somewhat like that of his horse, Scout, and somewhat less than Silver.

It not only is unfair to the Indian that he is portrayed thus. It also is unfortunate for those who really want to know what motivated Indians to go to war (other than being attacked by land-hungry whites). Let us look at another aspect of Indian warfare and the social makeup of some of the Southern Plains tribes: the organization of military and social societies that provided the Indian opportunity to achieve status and recognition among his people.

Though military societies were instrumental in organizing war expeditions, it was not their sole function. Some method of maintaining order in the camp, on the hunt, or in time of attack was needed. Most tribes therefore had what is usually called a soldier society whose job was to serve as the camp police. They were sometimes asked to intervene in cases of murder, destruction of property, or breaking of some village law. They were also on hand during the buffalo hunt so that order might be maintained. The greatest number of buffalo had to be killed before any individual frightened the animals away in his desire to be the first one to make the kill. The soldier societies had different names depending on the tribe. The Iowa called them The Braves; the Kansa, *Akida*; the Ponca, *Wanuce*; the Pawnee, *raripakusu* ("fighting for order"); the Kiowa, *K'oitsenko*, or "Chief Dogs." Possibly the most famous were the Crazy Dogs of the Cheyenne. Of the nomadic tribes it appears that only the Comanche were without any military society, suggesting a strong dependence on the individual's prowess as warrior or hunter rather than on a team effort.

Holding Eagle Tail, a Comanche police chief, photographed by Hutchins and Lanney in 1891. (*Smithsonian Institution*)

George Arkeketah, an Oto, wears two peace medals which were given to Indian leaders as a token of friendship by many U.S. Presidents. The photo was made by William Dinwiddie in 1895. (*Smithsonian Institution*)

There were also ceremonial and social organizations which had nothing to do with war per se, but whose members might be prominent warriors. We find one particular association, the Helushka (or Hedushka) among the Siouan speakers and Irushka among the Pawnee, a popular dance and ceremonial association which still survives today. Men and women both might participate in these associations. There were also associations exclusively for women which served the same purpose as a trade guild. Most of the women's associations were dedicated to crafts and learning skills necessary to fulfill their role in tribal society.

Some of the societies were organized by age. A young man might be invited to join a society of warriors until he reached an older age, at which time he would be asked to join another composed of older members. Some societies were limited to the older chiefs of the tribe. Others were exclusively for children. One such children's society found among the Kiowa was called the Rabbits.

The Rabbits, or *Tsanyup*, were made up of boys of ages ten to twelve and were under the leadership of two adults who belonged to other warrior societies. The prime obligation of the leaders was to the Rabbits, however. The Rabbits were much like a training school for warriors. The leaders taught the younger boys about warfare by recounting their own deeds of valor. If one of the adults died or was killed in battle, the other would nominate a new co-leader. The Rabbits had a particular kind of dance in which they placed their hands alongside their head to represent the ears of a rabbit and danced by jumping up and down in place. At the same time they would cry out *tsa, tsa*, imitating the sounds of the rabbit. This song and dance, even though it is very old, is still remembered by the Kiowa today, and often an old man will sing for the young to dance, even though the society has been officially disbanded.

The *K'oitsenko*, or "Chief Dogs," held the highest prestige among the Kiowa. Members were usually twenty-five years of age or more and wore a distinctive emblem, a sash which trailed to the ground. In battle the *K'oitsenko* staked their sash to the ground with a spear and were not allowed to retreat unless another member of the society released the spear. This particular practice was found among almost all tribes of the Southern Plains, as well as the Northern Highlands. The Omaha and Ponca had similar societies called Not Afraid to Die.

Men went on the warpath for a variety of reasons. Some went to avenge a relative's death at the hands of a hostile tribe. Others went to elevate their status. Alanson Skinner, a famous ethnographer who worked among the Iowa, Kansa, and Ponca, and published his research in the American Museum of Natural History's *Anthropological Papers*, says of the Iowa that their chief objective in going to war was to achieve fame. "A father might say to his son," writes Skinner, " 'Go out and die so that I may hear of you till the end of my days. Increase your name. If you are shot in the back and fall on your face, I'll be ashamed, but if you are wounded in front and fall on your back, I'll be proud.' "

Many Iowa slipped out at dawn to hit the trail armed only with sticks or no weapons at all, intent on being killed in battle. The Iowa also had an elaborate system of grading war exploits. Each grade had a title describing the deed accomplished, and the individual sought to attain these various titles. The highest honor was to be called *Wac'e*, or "successful partisan"—the leader who had conducted a number of successful war parties. The second honor was *Wabothage*, or "foe killer," given to a man who had slain many enemies. The third honor was divided equally among those who counted coup, an act in which a man armed only with a bow or coup stick struck an enemy and retreated without being killed; those who cut heads—either by riding and making the motion of severing the head, or if time was available, actually beheading the victims; those who scalped; and those who cut off a lock of hair from their victims.

Among the Ponca, the leader of the war party carried a *waxube*, or "war bundle," and set out ahead of the main group. If other members of the party saw the foe first, the leader had to be pointed in the direction of the enemy as he could neither retreat nor deviate in any manner from the path ahead of him. The bundle owner usually slept alone when the party was out, while an attendant prepared his food and served it to him.

When a Ponca killed an enemy, the victim was scalped and often the head severed and thrown away. Often they slashed the enemy's back in a checkerboard design which they called "making a drum of an enemy's back."

In addition to the soldier and warrior societies there were a number of bundle societies among the Caddoan and Siouan tribes. The entire social and political organization of the Pawnee, for example, was centered on the use of sacred bundles. Among the *Skidi*, each of the thirteen villages had a sacred bundle. In turn, there were bundle societies within the villages, such as the Two Lance Society, Red Lance Society, the Black Heads, and the Brave Ravens. There were no age restrictions in these societies, and a man could belong to all societies at once if he chose. Membership was for life. Each society had its own particular manner of dressing, its own emblems and badges of office, songs and dances, religious paraphernalia. Also, of course, it had the ever important sacred bundle which contained various consecrated items, such as the skins and feathers of birds, pipes, and other ceremonial objects. The bundle societies often served several functions—they might exclusively align for war, or serve as soldiers during a buffalo hunt or camp movement.

James Murie, the Pawnee anthropologist who did a great deal of research among his own people, describes an unusual bundle society of the Pawnee called the Crow Lance.

The Pawnee call this society *hatuka*, or "those coming behind," which refers to their custom of taking their place at the rear of the tribe as it moved on the hunt or in war. As in the case of most societies, its origin was in a dream. Long ago, a hunter was walking along a ravine when suddenly he heard the war cries of his enemies. He became frightened and quickly notched an arrow into his bowstring, although he could not yet see the enemy. The cries seemed to be coming from two sides, and he prepared to shoot the first enemy to show his face. Finally they appeared, but to his surprise they were not humans but flocks of crows, blackbirds, and a pack of wolves. The birds flew up into a formation resembling a lance. Then the man fell asleep and began to dream. The birds and animals told him that they had been testing his bravery and were about to give him a lance and teach him songs and rituals which would become the foundation of the Crow Lance Society.

When the man awoke, he collected the feathers of the crows and certain medicines which he would need. He returned home and prayed to Tirawahat, the Pawnee deity, and soon fell asleep again. This time he dreamed of a line of men attached together by means of a buffalo rope slipped through their belts. They were daubed with soot and taught him many songs. When he awoke, he taught a song to a companion, then fell asleep to learn more songs, which he taught other members of the society.

When the society was formed, the members made a lance from ash, covered with buffalo skin and crow feathers. They also made a buffalo rope like that worn by the men in the dream. As each new member joined he was required to attach a crow feather to the lance, an emblem of his bravery. As an initiation for new members, the society pretended they were attacking an enemy. The new members, along with older ones, were tied together by means of the buffalo rope. As the members marched forward singing, they began to twist the rope around the new members, causing the novices to be chafed. Those who could not bear the pain were admitted cowards and dismissed from the society. Those who unflinchingly underwent the ordeal became members and were feasted.

During the camp moves the Crow Lance marched behind the tribe. Should they be attacked by enemies, they would quickly string themselves together by means of the buffalo rope and fight. If a member was killed, he was dragged around amid the battle by the other members. It is said that, finally, during one battle all the members of the Crow Lance were killed. Later, another tried to reorganize the society by making a new Crow Lance, but was attacked by the enemy and the lance was taken from him. Since that time, the Crow Lance Society has been discontinued, and the last act to rejuvenate it is considered an evil omen.

In addition to the military and bundle societies there were a host of social and ceremonial associations, many for the sole purpose of conducting religious functions or secular feasts and dances. Probably the most popular of the latter which has been revived today is the Helushka Society. This society was found among all the Siouan speakers, though the name changes slightly in pronunciation (Hedushka) depending on the tribe, and is also known among the Pawnee as the Irushka. The names and ceremonies of this society are so similar that it was undoubtedly diffused from one tribe to another and quite possibly had its origin among the Pawnee, though some experts place its origin among the Ponca and Omaha. The Pawnee, Ponca, Osage, and Oto-Missouri still observe many ceremonies of the Hedushka today in their popular straight dances held every year.

The oldest form of the society is the Pawnee Irushka and its main function is religious. The name *Irushka* means "they are inside the fire" (but commonly translated "warrior") and pertains to a dream by the originator of the society. In the dream he discovered humans dipping their hands into boiling water and playing with fire, laughing as they did so. They told the man they had a new dance to teach him and proceeded to hold him over hot coals which caused him to scream. Suddenly he discovered that he no longer felt pain from the fire. After this the humans taught him the songs and rituals he would need to organize the Irushka—then they turned into birds and animals and left.

The man did not sleep well that night because he dreamed of the fire ordeal. The next day he went out on a hill to fast and met a man who asked him to follow him. They came to a place where the same humans of the dream were sitting around a fire singing and laughing. Again he was given the fire ordeal, and again the humans turned into birds and animals and disappeared. But this time one man stayed. He said that in a fight he had lost his scalp lock and could never go back to his people because of the disgrace. Some birds and animals, however, had taught him to make a headdress from deer hair, turkey, and eagle feathers that resembled a scalp lock. The deer hair was woven together to resemble a roached mane; in the middle was placed a spreader made from the shoulder blade of a deer. A two-inch shank bone was placed on the spreader and an eagle feather inserted into it. The birds and animals also taught the man how to make other articles of costume to be worn in the dances. All these things he gave to the initiate, who in turn taught the ceremonies to his people. The headdress, today called a roach, represented the fire ordeal of the Irushka. The red deer hair represented the fire, and the black hair, smoke. The bone shank represented the special medicine given to the originator, and the eagle feather represented the man himself standing in the middle of the fireplace. In addition to the headdress, the man was given bustle feathers called a crow belt.

While the symbolism came from the Pawnee, the actual organization of the Irushka, or—as it was called later by other tribes—the Hedushka, was greatly influenced by the Osage and Omaha. There were a number of formal positions occupied in the Hedushka, including the owner of the drum, the leaders of the society, the singers, male and female, tail dancers, whip bearers, and a number of lay members. Each officer of the society occupied a specific place at the Hedushka dance, which was later held inside a multisided dance house. When the singers began, the whip bearers, sometimes called starters, got up to dance as a signal for the rest to follow. Sometimes the whip bearers would actually whip those who refrained from dancing with the special emblem of their office, a whip made of wood resembling the hind leg of a rabbit.

Among many tribes, the fire ordeal learned by the Pawnee was reenacted. Dancers would line up and dance by a kettle of boiling meat and thrust their hands into the water. It is said they rubbed their hands and forearms with a special medicine that prevented them from being scalded. At the end of each dance, a man singled out for his bravery would be elected to dance the tail, or encore of the dance, alone. During the Hedushka dances there was much speechmaking and giving away of blankets and horses and other gifts, and the dance was always concluded with a feast. Among some tribes dogs were ceremonially cooked and eaten.

The Osage have always been credited with adhering closest to the old form of the dance which they perform alternately at Gray Horse, Hominy, and Pawhuska. In the mid-fifties, the Ponca decided to revive the Hedushka Society and today are called upon to sing at most of the straight dances held in Oklahoma. Most of the Indians agree that the Ponca songs are closest to the old-time songs originally sung for the Hedushka dances.

In addition to men's societies, women had their own associations which they formed for the purpose of learning crafts, or for religious and secular performances. Probably one of the most popular dances which still survives today under a different name is the scalp dance, performed by female relatives of warriors. The women carried the trophies of their male relatives tied to sticks in this dance while the warriors sang. Today the scalp dance, minus the trophies, is called the round dance and is one of the most popular in Oklahoma.

While most of the societies that existed up to the turn of the present century have all but disappeared, there has been interest on the part of some tribes to reorganize the old associations. As mentioned before, the

Ponca have taken renewed interest in the Hedushka Society. In addition, the Kiowa and Kiowa Apache have also reorganized two older societies. Among the Kiowa, the society is known as the Black Legging Society. In the old days the Black Legging had two leaders, one of whom carried a crooked lance covered with beaver skin and eagle feathers. During a skirmish, the lance bearer stuck it in the ground and could not retreat unless a comrade removed it for him. The society lay dormant for a number of years but was reinstated in the fifties.

I witnessed a Black Legging Society dance in 1960 in which members wore black tights and fringed shawls wrapped around in the fashion of kilts. They danced in a straight line, one member carrying a crooked lance, stepping in place in time to the music. During the dance a veteran of World War II narrated his exploits over the public-address system in the Kiowa language, which was translated by the master of ceremonies.

The society has its counterpart among the Kiowa Apache who call their association the Black Feet Society, and is restricted to veterans of foreign wars. The Kiowa also have a dance society called the Ohomo— which is probably a corruption of the word "Omaha" —into which members of various tribes are accepted. The function of the Ohomo is primarily social, and only the best dancers belong. The women's societies have for the most part been replaced by War Mother's Clubs similar to non-Indian associations for women. The War Mothers often help sponsor public dances and perform in the ceremonies as a unit. They usually wear fringed shawls bearing patriotic emblems or the names of their sons, their divisions, and campaigns embroidered on them.

Since the Indian has had a resurgence of interest in the old ways, it can be predicted that the old social organizations will continue to play an important role in his modern world.

6

Famous People

THE AMERICAN Indians who have achieved no-
tice in history books or artistic circles have largely been
men and women who found success in a white man's
world. The criterion for being well known or famous
has historically been whether or not the Indian in question has adjusted to the white man's rules and regulations of civilization and how far he has progressed
within the framework of these rules.

It is not surprising, then, to find that among the most
successful Indians are listed Charles Curtiss, Vice Pres-
ident of the United States, under Herbert Hoover, who
was descended from Kansa and Osage leaders; Major
General Clarence Tinker, of Osage descent, who played
an important part in World War II by reorganizing the
U.S. Air Force after the Japanese attack on Pearl Har-
bor; the Tallchief sisters, Maria and Marjorie, also
Osage, who became well-known ballerinas; and N. Scott
Momaday, the 1969 recipient of the Pulitzer Prize for
fiction, who is Kiowa.

To this list could be added a number of Indians who

have achieved success in business—especially in the state of Oklahoma. While one cannot deny the right of any man to seek his vocation wherever he feels qualified, whether it be in the white man's world or the Indian's, it would be grossly unfair not to consider famous those persons who were considered leaders *as* Indians as well as *by* Indians. This list is not so well known. Their names rarely appear in standard history books, and when they do, they are often portrayed unrealistically. They are known to only a few specialists, and, of course, the Indian people themselves. They have a few things in common: They remained leaders only as long as they represented the best interests of their people; they never delegated to others those things which they could not do themselves; and in the broad picture of late nineteenth-century confrontation with the whites, they were forced to choose between living as whites or Indians. No matter what their choice, they often met with a tragic ending, treacherously murdered or exiled.

Whether to remain Indian and be destroyed by white soldiers, or to follow the dictates of Washington and live a bleak life on the reservation was often the dilemma of Indian leaders. Some continued to fight to the death, others tried to compromise. Compromise often meant only temporary shelter from the white soldiers and often the repudiation by one's own tribe for selling out to the whites. The highest price paid was often by the leader himself.

Black Kettle was a famous leader of the Southern Cheyennes who by 1853 had proved himself brave against the Kiowa, Comanche, and Pawnee. White gold miners had invaded his country in the vast stretches of Colorado. It was inevitable that his warriors would soon fight the white men crazed by the yellow metal. But Black Kettle, with foresight of what would eventually happen to his people and country, tried to prevent hostilities. Telling his people not to fight the whites, he went in good faith to Fort Lyon to discuss the problem with the governor of the territory. Black Kettle stopped thirty miles from the fort and camped on Sand Creek. To show his loyalty to the United States, he raised an American flag above his tepee. It was in this camp that the wise old man with deep-set eyes and a slight frown studied the eventualities confronting his people and the consequences of a treaty.

On a cold November morning in 1864, the pistol shots and shrieks of Colonel J. M. Chivington's Colorado Volunteers cut through Black Kettle's peaceful camp. Taken completely by surprise, Black Kettle, half dazed by the incredulity of the episode, tried desperately to escape the bullets and hacking swords of the cavalrymen. Blindly trying to flee up a frozen creek bed, he saw his people massacred before his eyes. Men, women, and children were mercilessly murdered as they tried to escape. Black Kettle, half in disbelief, watched his own wife shot to death as they scrambled for safety. He heard the pleas of the women and children begging for mercy as the hardened Volunteers shot them down with deliberate aim.

Black Kettle, though reported dead, escaped. More than a hundred of his tribesmen were horribly scalped and mutilated by the white troops. More than a hundred Indian scalps were taken to Denver and exhibited in triumph between acts of a theatrical event. Eyewitness accounts told how the soldiers with little emotion blew the brains out of small children and cut the unborn fetuses out of pregnant women with their bloodied sabers.

Everyone asked, why such a massacre? Hatred, pure hatred, was the answer. But no official in Washington took any action, despite the criticism of whites who normally condoned the wholesale killing of Indians. It was a cold-blooded program against the peaceful Cheyenne, one more easily forgotten than defended. For a few weeks Black Kettle, his survivors, and allied Arapaho blocked the gold trail across Colorado. The Sand Creek Massacre could not be dismissed by the Indians who saw it as easily as it was by Washington bureaucrats. No white dared tread across that area of Indian country. Black Kettle tried desperately to find a way that would enable his people to live, but it was hopeless. More and more whites came, and more and more Indians died. Finally, in 1865, Black Kettle, still having faith in peaceful negotiations with the government, signed another treaty. The conditions of the treaty which guaranteed free hunting provisions and annuities were completely ignored by the United States. At this point his own people began to lose faith in Black Kettle. But he was a powerful man and soon regained a following.

At this point he joined with other tribes and signed the famous Medicine Lodge Treaty of 1867. The treaty provided again for land and assurance that the tribes could retire to reservations in Indian Territory and live at peace with the United States—a relatively small crumb to throw to the tired, starving people who once owned all the land. Physically and morally defeated, Black Kettle might have had the chance to abide by the terms of the treaty except for one more episode instigated by a newcomer to Indian country—a white military leader whose name would be known for generations to come as the foremost Indian fighter. He was young, ambitious, and a hero of the Civil War. His name was Custer.

George Armstrong Custer had become the youngest

general in the Union Army at the age of twenty-three.
Born in Ohio and a graduate of West Point, he had
achieved a reputation at the battles of Manassas and
Gettysburg. At the end of the Civil War he elected to
go West and fight Indians. He arrived in Kansas in
1867, but his early campaigns against the combined
forces of the Cheyenne, Arapaho, and Kiowa were un-
fruitful. His experience as an officer in the Union Army
had not given him the necessary talent to fight Indians.
He could not match the skill of the Indians in an open
fight. His solution was to surprise them in their winter
camp, attack when they least suspected.

In November, 1868, there were some isolated cases of
Indians raiding farmhouses and stealing cattle. This
was the excuse Custer wanted. Although terms of the
treaty stated that no tribes should be punished for the
hostilities of its individual members, Custer marched
against the peaceful camp of Black Kettle with orders
from his commanding officer, General Phil Sheridan, to
"destroy [the Indian] villages and ponies; to kill or
hang all warriors and bring back all women and children."

Custer and his famed Seventh Cavalry started toward
Black Kettle's village located on the Washita River. It
was November, almost four years to the day since the
Sand Creek Massacre, and it was dawn. A raging bliz-
zard had cast snow and ice around the peaceful village.
All at once the cry of "Soldiers!" echoed through the
camp. Custer had arrived, his bugler sounding the
charge followed by the Seventh's death song "Gar-
ryowen." It was Sand Creek all over again. Black Kettle
and his new wife quickly mounted a pony as the camp
scrambled to get out of the way of flying bullets. But
this time it was too late for the venerable chief. Among
the hundred or more Cheyenne men, women, and chil-

dren killed was Black Kettle, a man of peace who along with his wife died by the white man's bullet in what has been deviously recounted in history as the "Battle" of the Washita.

Satanta, sometimes called *Set'tainte*, or "White Bear," was one of the fiercest leaders of the proud Kiowa and one of the greatest orators of the Plains. White Bear, along with Lone Wolf and Kicking Bird, other famous Kiowa chiefs, was hated by Custer, who wanted to destroy all Indians. The Kiowa and Comanche allies gave Custer a particularly hard time on the Plains, one for which he sought retribution. It was not Custer, however, but another equally famous Indian fighter of the Southwest, Kit Carson, who first attacked the Kiowa, Comanche, and Cheyenne after they had been raising havoc in the Texas Panhandle. In 1864, under orders of General James H. Carleton, Carson and about 400 officers, troops, and Apache and Ute scouts began their march on the Indian villages near the old trading post called Adobe Walls. A fight broke out early in the morning. Carson, using howitzers, was able to destroy 176 Kiowa lodges and all their winter provisions. In the midst of the battle, White Bear confused the white soldiers by blowing a bugle captured from an earlier battle. As the U.S. bugler blew one call, White Bear blew an opposite call, thus adding more confusion to the turmoil. For the next few years, maddened by the fate of Black Kettle, White Bear and his Kiowa continued to raid against the Texans, Mexicans, and other whites.

White Bear attended the Medicine Lodge Treaty conference in 1867 bedecked in feathers and war paint. Though sixty years old, his spirit was young. In the midst of the dignified treaty signing, he suddenly blew his stolen bugle—greatly to the amusement of Indians and whites alike. But there was no amusement to White Bear when he made his mark on the paper which provided that the Kiowa and other tribes be settled in white men's houses. He wanted to remain free and not be herded onto a reservation like the white man's cattle.

Although the Medicine Lodge Treaty was an attempt to end all hostilities on the Southern Plains, few Indians who signed the paper had any faith in it. The memory of Black Kettle was still fresh in their minds, and anyway, they did not want to live in square houses and be denied the right to roam the Plains freely, as had been their custom. The great leaders signed the treaty, but to them it was just another piece of white man's paper.

Though the Kiowa had signed the Medicine Lodge Treaty, it did not prevent Custer from destroying Cheyenne and Kiowa villages. After the murder of Black Kettle, the Kiowa decided to surrender. White Bear himself, along with Lone Wolf, approached Custer's camp carrying white flags as a sign of truce. Custer immediately placed them under arrest and used them as hostages until the rest of the Kiowa surrendered. Fearful that their chiefs would be killed, the Kiowa obeyed. They surrendered at Fort Cobb and were later placed on a reservation at Fort Sill, Oklahoma.

But it was difficult to adjust to being confined to the boundaries of the reservation. The warriors sneaked off the reservation to hunt buffalo and eventually came into conflict with white settlers nearby. In 1871, White Bear also left, this time to raid the Texans who were building a railroad across his favorite hunting grounds. In one fight seven teamsters were killed.

When White Bear returned to the reservation, General William T. Sherman placed him and three other Kiowa—Lone Wolf, Sitting Bear, and Big Tree—under arrest for the murder of the teamsters. Lone Wolf escaped, but White Bear, Sitting Bear, and Big Tree were sent to Texas for trial. On the way Sitting Bear tried to escape and was killed by soldiers. White Bear and Big Tree were sentenced to be hanged to death, but their sentence was commuted to life imprisonment because the Indian agent felt their execution would cause a general uprising. Indeed, Lone Wolf, who had escaped, threatened war on the whites if White Bear was not released. He asked the Comanche and Cheyenne to join him on the warpath against the whites until their leaders were freed. Two years later White Bear and Big Tree were exonerated and brought back to Fort Sill.

Soon there were reports of more Indian raids in Texas. White Bear and Big Tree were blamed even though their whereabouts could be accounted for by their Indian agent. Big Tree had been sick at home; White Bear had been on a buffalo hunt. Nevertheless, White Bear was again arrested and sent to Texas to prison at Huntsville. Big Tree would have been imprisoned too, but he managed to disappear.

White Bear stayed in prison for two more years. If the confines of the reservation were too much restraint for this free-riding soul, the small cell must have been unbearable. White Bear became bitter and desperate. In the fall of 1876, while younger Indians back on the reservation chased buffalo across the prairie, White Bear gazed out of the tiny window of his cell at the open country he loved so much. Then he calmly slashed the arteries in his neck. As prison guards tried to rush him from prison to the hospital, White Bear leaped two stories to his death. Ironically, White Bear died the same year as the soldier who once held him hostage. A few months earlier, reports had come from the north country that the leader of the Seventh Cavalry had been slain by the Sioux at the Battle of the Little Big Horn. Custer, too, was dead.

It was customary among the Southern Plains tribes who raided in Texas and Mexico to take captives. The captives were sometimes killed, sometimes enslaved, but more often adopted by the tribes. Thus among the Southern Plains tribes are a great number of Spanish and English names.

During one raid by the Comanche in eastern Texas, a ten-year-old girl named Cynthia Ann Parker was captured by the powerful *Kwahadi* band. She grew up in the *Kwahadi* village and later married the band's chief, Nokoni. Their first son was born around 1845, and in the tradition of the Comanche was known by his mother's surname. His first name was Quanah. Quanah Parker was to grow up to be a great warrior and man of extraordinary vision.

During the early 1800's, the Comanche were generally friendly to most Americans, with the exception of the Texans who had encroached upon their best hunting grounds. In this warlike atmosphere of raids in Texas and Mexico, Quanah Parker grew to manhood. He became a fearless warrior and when his father died was elected chief, even though the Comanche did not usually consider the chieftainship hereditary. It was Quanah's forcefulness as a warrior and leader that earned him his title.

As leader of the most powerful band of Comanche, the *Kwahadi*, Quanah and his followers participated in all the major skirmishes on the Western Plains along with their Cheyenne and Kiowa allies. Quanah, like

White Bear and his Kiowa, the Kiowa Apache, Cheyenne, and Arapaho, was present at the signing of the
Medicine Lodge Treaty in Kansas. But Quanah did not
trust the white man and refused to sign the treaty. He
resolved never to be placed on a reservation and chose
to live on the Staked Plain along with other Indians
who refused to sign the treaty. His resolutions were
even stronger as he heard of the fate of Black Kettle and
White Bear. He would stay on the Staked Plain and
hunt buffalo.

But even his hunting grounds were not safe from the
enemy. White buffalo hunters began to deprive the Indian of his livelihood. This infuriated Quanah, who decided that in order to stop the white man a large and
powerful confederacy of tribes must be formed. He
called a great council on the North Fork of the Red
River and invited Lone Wolf's Kiowa, and Stone Calf's
Cheyenne.

Quanah's plan was first to drive out the buffalo hunters who were the most immediate threat to his people.
Stone Calf agreed, but Lone Wolf wanted to attack the
reservations and kill the agents and soldiers. Lone Wolf
finally acquiesced, and plans were made to attack the
buffalo hunters camped at Adobe Walls in the Texas
Panhandle.

On June 27, 1874, Quanah leading the Comanche,
Lone Wolf leading the Kiowa, and Stone Calf at the
head of the Cheyenne attacked Adobe Walls. They had
mustered some 700 warriors. At the post 30 buffalo
hunters lay asleep. It appeared this would be the first
victory for the combined forces of tribes. Had it not
been for an accident—the breaking of a ridge pole in the
fort which awakened one of the hunters—the Indians
might have swooped down on the whites and finished
them off. However, the hunter who was awakened real-

ized that his horse was alarmed. Then he saw hundreds of warriors riding full speed toward the fort. The buffalo hunters jumped to their feet and grabbed their weapons—high-powered, long-range rifles, unknown to the Indians. Firing swiftly and accurately, the hunters held off the Indians.

Quanah kept the battle going for three days, despite the fact he had been wounded and some of the best warriors killed. The new weapons were too much for him; the thick walls of the fort impenetrable. Quanah finally retreated to his camp. He had lost the final battle, a battle that signaled the end of the free-roving spirit of the Southern Plains Indians. Faced with retaliation from the U.S. Army or starvation on the Plains, Quanah Parker and his band of Comanche surrendered in the summer of 1875.

But Quanah, still young, was the respected leader of his people. Thinking about his white mother, who had learned the ways of the Indian, he decided that he too could learn new ways—those of the white man. First, he prevailed on the rest of the Comanche to come to the reservation. Some say that his real leadership began when he chose to follow the white man's road. For thirty years Quanah served as a spokesman and statesman for the Kiowa and Apache, as well as for his own tribe. He became interested in education for his people and encouraged them to learn how to farm. He was a shrewd businessman and taught his people to lease their land as pasture for additional income. He built himself a fine house and encouraged others to do so.

Quanah led a distinguished career. He spoke Spanish and English fluently, in addition to his native tongue. He was a frequent guest in Washington and rode in Theodore Roosevelt's inaugural parade. But Quanah, despite his grasp of the white man's way, remained a true Indian. According to Comanche custom, he had five wives. He was also instrumental in preserving the ancient beliefs and customs of his people. He was particularly active in the Native American Church, sometimes called the Peyote cult, and lived as one of the most highly esteemed members of his tribe. He died in 1911 when about seventy-six years old, and in 1957 his body was reinterred at the post cemetery at Fort Sill, Oklahoma, with full military honors. Half his life, he lived at war with the white man; the other half at peace. His decision must have been difficult. But in choosing the white man's way after suffering the white man's wrath, he tried to act for the benefit of his people.

7

Native Religion

THERE NEVER has been evidence of a case of human beings existing without a means of communication, a way of clothing themselves and educating their young to take their place in the tribe. There are no records of cultures that did not have some form of recreation, entertainment, music, or dance. And no matter how civilized or primitive these groups have been, all have asked themselves the questions: Why was I born and why must I die?

Every group has adequately answered these questions in the formation of a body of philosophy which we commonly call religion. If the doctrines of these religions do not coincide with the preachments of the recognized religions of the civilized world, there has been a tendency to characterize them as primitive religion or paganism.

These facts are evident in what I prefer to call native religion as it applies to some of the Southern Plains tribes. The term "native" simply means that the religion predated the teachings of Christianity which came to the New World as part of the overall civilizing process administered by the white man. Although the early Spanish and French missionaries who first traveled among the Southern Plains tribes found the Indian religions to be "paganistic rituals," the religious beliefs of the Indians were, in fact, highly sophisticated and were rich in doctrine.

Ceremonies designed to ask the supreme deities to look out for the welfare of the entire tribe often lasted for days or even weeks. While there were many formal ceremonies such as the sun dance in which numerous persons participated in view of the entire village, native Indian religion was basically the responsibility of the individual. A man could go through life satisfying his religious needs without ever participating in a congregational form of worship.

The vision quest mentioned earlier was of primary importance to the Indian in obtaining a guardian spirit, which took the form of an animal, bird, or inanimate object. Certain men, through these visions, often became shamans or medicine men, men who could lead religious ceremonies and had the power to make predictions and interpret other men's visions. The shaman was an important member of the tribe, capable of curing sickness, finding lost objects, and in general acting as an intermediary between the common man and the spirits.

As might be expected, the sedentary tribes that lived in permanent villages had more time on their hands to involve themselves in things other than pure survival. It is not surprising, therefore, to find among the non-nomadic tribes a particularly rich religious practice. The Pawnee seem to have been great innovators. It was true in their religion, which some believe one of the most comprehensive philosophies of all peoples.

Wichita dance leaders hold corn and pipe, symbolic in the Indian tradition of what was given to them at the beginning of the world. The man wears a ghost dance shirt, which, many Indians believed in the latter part of the nineteenth century, made one invincible to white man's bullets. This photo was taken by James Mooney around 1892. (*Smithsonian Institution*)

As did all Indians, the Pawnee had a love of stories which described the creation of the world, the origin of man, and the power of the gods. The Pawnee believed that Tirawa was the Supreme Being. Tirawa was married to the Vault of Heaven, and both reigned somewhere in the heavens in a place beyond the clouds. Yet they were purely spiritual beings and took no earthly shape. Tirawa sent his commands to mankind through a series of lesser gods and messengers who personified themselves to the Pawnee.

Next in importance to Tirawa and his wife was *Tcuperika*, the "Evening Star," personified as a young maiden. The Evening Star was keeper of a garden in the west which was the source of all food. She had four assistants, the Wind, the Cloud, Lightning, and Thunder. In Pawnee mythology she married the next important deity, *Opirikata*, the "Morning Star," and from them was born the first being on earth. The Morning Star was conceived as a strong warrior who drove the rest of the stars before him. In some of the Pawnee ceremonies, a human sacrifice—a young captive girl— was offered to him. Later the practice was put to an end by their great chief Petalasharo of the *Skidi* band.

Below the Evening and Morning stars were the lesser gods of the four directions—the Northeast, Southeast, Southwest, and Northwest—and next in rank to the four directions were the three gods of the North: the North Star, chief of all the stars; the North Wind, who gave the buffalo to mankind; and Hikus, who gave life itself to men. Next in line came the Sun and the Moon who likewise were married and produced an offspring who became the second person on earth. It was the marriage of this second person with the offspring of the Evening and Morning stars that began the race of mankind on earth.

There were lesser gods, most of them stars, who also played roles in Pawnee philosophy. The Star of the South, for instance, stood at the southern end of the Milky Way, made up of the campfires of the departed, and received the spirits of the dead. It is also believed that another star called *Skiritiuhuts*, or "Fool Wolf," became offended at one of the councils of the star people and in revenge introduced death to mankind.

Not only were the philosophy and mythology of the Pawnee rich, but their ceremonies were many and varied. There were ceremonies to the Thunder, the Morning and Evening stars, for the planting and harvesting of Mother Corn, as well as lesser ceremonies. One of the best documented is a ceremony called the Hako which was investigated by a well-known anthropologist, Alice C. Fletcher, during the early 1880's and subsequently published by the Bureau of American Ethnology in Washington, D.C.

As to the purpose of the ceremony, Miss Fletcher writes: "The ceremony of the Hako is a prayer for children, in order that the tribe may increase and be strong; and also that the people may have long life, enjoy plenty, and be happy and at peace."

The ceremony was conducted by a man called *Kurahus*, meaning "man of years," who was venerated for his knowledge and experience. To him was entrusted the supervision of all ceremonies and songs which had to be performed in precisely the same order each time. There was no exact time for the Hako to be performed, but it was never done in the winter. As one Pawnee said, "We take up the Hako in the spring when the birds are mating, or in the summer when the birds are nesting and caring for their young, or the fall when the birds are flocking, but not in the winter when all things are asleep. With the Hako we are praying for the gift of life, or strength, of plenty, and of peace, so we must pray when life is stirring everywhere."

The people who took part in the ceremony were divided into two groups, the fathers who sponsored the ceremony, and the children who received the intentions, prayers, and gifts from the fathers. The head of the fathers' group, called father, was responsible for employing the *Kurahus* who were familiar with the songs and rituals. The head of the children's group, called son, also played an important part in the ceremony in acting on behalf of all the children.

The most important paraphernalia used in the Hako were the sacred, feathered stems resembling pipestems without the bowls. The ceremony took three days and three nights during which time twenty-seven rituals were performed, each ritual and song unveiling to the participants the sacred lore of the Pawnee. At the end of the ceremony the feathered wands were waved over the children, thus indicating and sealing a bond between the fathers and children which was stronger than blood tie. At the end of the ceremony most of the ritual paraphernalia was cast away, except for the feathered stems which were given to one of the children for his keeping. At a later date the children might take the part of the fathers and offer the prayers to another group of children, thus perpetuating the ceremony and the residual solidarity of the tribe. It is said that the children might also take the feathered stems to groups from other tribes and thus insure peace between the Pawnee and other Indians.

Another religious convocation, usually performed in the early summer and widespread among all Plains tribes, was the sun dance. It owes its name to the fact that certain men who had taken vows participated in this dance gazing at the sun, dancing for several days with-

Young Southern Cheyenne warriors on horseback with a sun dance lodge in the background. Photographed by Lanney on the Cheyenne Reservation in 1892. (*Smithsonian Institution*)

out food or water. In some cases the dancers had skewers of wood placed through the fleshy part of their chest and attached to rawhide thongs suspended from a pole. They danced until the flesh broke loose, freeing them from the sun dance pole.

Some tribes such as the Kiowa did not employ self-torture. In the Kiowa version of the sun dance, a man who owned a *taime*, or "sacred doll," alone could decide to sponsor a sun dance. The medicine doll, which represented a kind of war medicine, was hung in the medicine lodge where the dance was to be held. The Kiowa name for the dance was *K'othun*, which refers to this particular lodge.

The man who owned the *taime* became the director of the dance and principal performer. Others who wished to dance the sun dance were required to make vows to the *taime*, which was kept outside the keeper's tepee and only exposed during the dance. James Mooney, who did much research among the Kiowa, describes the doll as "a small image, less than two feet in length, representing a human figure dressed in a robe of white feathers, with a headdress consisting of a single upright feather and pendants of ermine skin, with numerous strands of blue beads around its neck, and painted upon the face, breast, and back with designs symbolic of the sun and moon. . . . The image itself is of dark-green stone, in form rudely resembling a human head and bust. . . . It is preserved in a rawhide box . . . and is never under any circumstances exposed to view except at the annual sun dance, when it is fastened to a short upright stick planted within the medicine lodge, near the western side. . . ."

Three classes of dancers were allowed to sun dance in addition to the leader: the associates, the shield keepers, and the common dancers. Each class painted their faces and bodies differently and wore different-colored clothing. The leader, it is said, dressed to represent the *taime*. The dancers danced barefoot with long kilts and wrist bands and anklets of sage. Each carried an eagle bone whistle which he blew in time with the singing and drumming. Even without the self-torture, the sun dance was a particularly strenuous ordeal, for the dancers had to gaze constantly at the sun as they danced. They were allowed no food or water and rested only at nighttime. During the dancing many of them had visions which were later interpreted by shamans.

Because of the self-torture practiced in the sun dance by many tribes, the ceremony was prohibited by law in the latter 1890's. It was never renewed on the Southern Plains, although many Northern Plains tribes since the 1930's have revived it. Many of the Southern Cheyenne and Arapaho go North each year to witness the dance performed by their Northern kin. This does not mean that native religion is dead on the Southern Plains. There is at least one ceremony which is very old that brings the Northerners down to Oklahoma even to this day. It is the sacred arrow renewal ceremony of the Cheyenne.

The Cheyenne believe that long ago their Supreme Being, Maiyun, gave four sacred arrows to the mythological hero Sweet Medicine in a large cave in what is now the Black Hills of South Dakota. Maiyun taught Sweet Medicine that two of the arrows had supernatural power over the buffalo and the other two over human beings. Maiyun instructed the young man in the proper care and ceremonies connected with the arrows and charged Sweet Medicine with the responsibility of teaching the Cheyenne about their mysterious powers.

Sweet Medicine taught the Cheyenne that the two arrows used for buffalo would be helpful in hunting. All that needed to be done was to point the two sacred arrows at the buffalo before the hunt and it would cause the buffalo to be helpless and easier to kill. In the same manner Sweet Medicine taught the people that pointing the two arrows used for humans at the enemy before battle would cause them to be blinded, confused, and vulnerable to defeat by the Cheyenne warriors.

The Cheyenne say that from the time Sweet Medicine taught their people the ritual of the sacred arrows, the arrows have been carefully kept in a fox skin bundle, which has been handed down from one generation to another and guarded by a special man known as the sacred arrow keeper. In alternate years an individual pledges to sponsor an arrow renewal ceremony and the arrows are unwrapped and displayed to all the male members of the tribe. The man making the pledge does so in order to fulfill a vow, such as is the case in the sun dance. The vow was originally made when a warrior was threatened during a fight or became sick and was fearful of dying. Although only one person makes the pledge, the entire ceremony is given in behalf of all the Cheyenne people so that they will be insured of a long and prosperous life.

The renewal ceremony traditionally takes four days to perform. A special lodge in which the ceremony is to take place is prepared on the first day. Warriors held in high esteem by their tribe are selected to choose the spot on which the lodge will be erected. New poles are cut and the lodge covering borrowed from families of good reputation. Inside the lodge the priests of the tribe will sit on sage during the ceremony. As part of the preparation, each Cheyenne family gives a special counting stick to the conductor of the ceremony. Symbolically, the sticks represent each member of the Cheyenne tribe.

On the second day the sacred arrows are obtained from the keeper, and the bundle is opened and examined. If the flight feathers of the arrows are in any way damaged, a man known for his bravery and generosity is chosen to replace the feathers. On the third day the arrows are renewed, and each of the counting sticks is passed over incense to bless all the families in the tribes. On the last day the arrows are exposed to the male members of the tribe. The Cheyenne say that it is difficult to look at the arrows because they give off a blinding light. To conclude the ceremony, the Cheyenne priests make predictions about the future of their people. After all have taken a sweat bath, the renewal ceremony is officially over and the Cheyenne figuratively begin life over.

A respect for and a fear of ghosts were both central to many Indian beliefs. It was believed, and still is by some, that spirits of the departed freely roam the earth. The spirits are capable of both helping and harming mortals. Some birds and animals are regarded as having the same powers as bad spirits and are avoided if at all possible. Such is true of the owl and yellowhammer. Among the Pawnee, both birds are associated with witchcraft. The Pawnee tell of a chief's son who was killed by witches in order to obtain the fat from his heart to keep in their witch bundles. The chief powers of the witches, they say, were derived from the owl and yellowhammer. The witches revealed to the chief that they had killed his son by shooting an owl's claw and yellowhammer feather into his son's heart through their magical powers. In revenge of his son's death, the chief burned the witches and their bundles, thus destroying their power. Today many Indians are afraid to travel alone at night for fear that they will be confronted by witches.

Comanche, for example, will not even touch an owl feather. Others believe that witches still exist and may take over the control of one's will by gazing into his eyes. It is common at many Indian dances held around Oklahoma for contest dancers to wear witch paint, a stripe of red paint over both eyes. They say that a witch may prevent them from winning a dance contest by gazing into their eyes, which will cause them to stumble in the dance, or some way else be eliminated. The dancers say that the red paint across their eyes will distract anyone from gazing directly into their eyes and thus acts as a witch repellent, much as wolf bane was used in Europe to ward off werewolves. But just as owls and yellowhammers are dangerous, eagles and flickers are considered sacred and bring good luck. Many Indians carry two flicker feathers in their pocket for good luck.

Just as certain men could become shamans by fasting and praying, there were also powerful medicine women. Their power, like the men's, was received in visions. Wonderful feats of curing were often attributed to these medicine women.

A Comanche once told me about a relative of hers who was hemorrhaging from the mouth. Instead of calling a white doctor, the Comanche sent for an old medicine woman. The medicine woman called for a frying pan in which she placed cedar incense. As the patient lay hemorrhaging the woman took a black scarf from her bag and began to pray. As she prayed she tied a knot in the scarf. Slowly the hemorrhaging subsided a little. She tied another knot, and still another, each time causing the hemorrhaging to subside. By the time she had tied the fourth knot the hemorrhaging had completely stopped and the patient was cured.

Although the missionaries successfully indoctrinated many Indian people into the white man's religion, there was one last attempt to revive Indian religion in the latter part of the nineteenth century. In the state of Nevada a Paiute Indian named Wovoka dreamed that the white man would disappear from the face of the earth and that all the Indians who had died would return to the earth. The buffalo would also come back and the tribes would return to the old way of life. In his vision he claimed he visited with the spirits of the deceased Indians and they taught him a dance that would bring the destruction of the white man through natural means. Wovoka claimed it was useless to fight the white man any longer and that the Indians would live in peace, for soon a cataclysmic event would take place that would kill only white people. Wovoka was considered an Indian messiah, and the name of his preachment was soon to be known as the ghost dance.

The ghost dance spread rapidly throughout the Plains. On the Southern Plains, the Apache, Cheyenne, Arapaho, Caddo, Pawnee, Wichita, Kiowa, Kiowa Apache, as well as all the Siouan speakers, took up the new doctrine. Only the Comanche did not adhere to it, preferring their own individual form of religion. In the dance, the dancers danced for long hours until some fainted and went into trances where they had visions. Upon awakening, they sang songs telling about their visits to the spirit land and how soon the old way of life would return.

James Mooney, an ethnologist from the Bureau of American Ethnology, was present at many ghost dances and recorded a number of songs and prayers. He writes of a pathetic ghost dance song that was sung by an Arapaho, which caused the dancers to cry over their present conditions on the reservations. The song went:

> Father, have pity on me,
> Father, have pity on me;
> I am crying for thirst,
> I am crying for thirst;
> All is gone—I have nothing to eat,
> All is gone—I have nothing to eat.

Mooney recorded another song by a Cheyenne named Little Woman who was a leader in the ghost dance. She had been in many trances and composed many songs about what she had seen in her visions. In one she tells of the old game of shinny which she played with her friend:

> My comrade—Iyahe-yahe-e
> My comrade—Iyahe-yahe-e
> Let us go and play shinny—Ahe-e-ye
> Let us go and play shinny—Ahe-e-ye
> Let us look for our mother—Ahe-e-ye
> Let us look for our mother—Ahe-e-ye
> Our father tells us to do it—Ahe-e-ye
> Our father tells us to do it—Ahe-e-ye.

The Caddo sang of a great reunion of the living and the dead after the white man would be gone. Mooney records:

> Come on, Caddo, we are all going up,
> Come on, Caddo, we are all going up
> To the great village—he-e-ye
> To the great village—he-e-ye
> With our father above,
> With our father above where he dwells on high—he-e-ye
> Where our mother dwells—he-e-ye
> Where our mother dwells—he-e-ye

But the cataclysm did not come. The white man remained and the Indians suffered on the reservations from malnutrition and broken spirit. The Christian missionaries continued to proselytize and win many converts. But native religion was still to remain with the old people. Also a new religion was to spring up, a religion which had existed in Central America before the whites arrived and was soon to move rapidly through the Southwest and Plains. The religion had traces of Christianity, for the Indians prayed to Jesus Christ. But they did so in their own way, a way different from the church worship they had been forced to adopt. The new religion which was soon to be adopted by over half the Indians in the United States was called Peyotism.

8

Half Moon and Cross Fire

LONG BEFORE Columbus arrived in the New World, the Indians of Mexico were using a sacred plant of the cactus family in their religious rituals. The Aztec called it *peyotl*, referring to a number of plants that have elements producing hallucinatory sensations. These effects which accompany the eating of peyote—as it is called in the United States—in a green or dried state, or the drinking of peyote tea have caused the Indians to regard peyote as a sacred plant, a gift of a Supreme Deity which may be consumed for the welfare of the people during prayer meetings.

Since peyote is classified as a hallucinogenic drug, there has been a great deal of controversy over Indians' using the plant in their religious meetings. But both legal and moral implications (in the white man's sense) have not stopped Peyotism—or, as it is now called, the Native American Church—from becoming one of the most important Indian religions in the United States and Canada. The majority of Peyotists are found among the Southern Plains tribes, though members of almost all tribes in the United States and Canada belong.

The peyote plant is found in Mexico and Texas along the Rio Grande. From the tribes in Mexico the use of peyote, which in the early reports of missionaries and ethnographers was called the Peyote cult, made its way northward to the Apache, Tonkawa, Kiowa, Comanche, Cheyenne, and Arapaho, and ultimately to all neighboring tribes. To this day, Indians make the trip to the Mexican border to dig the radishlike plants and transport them back to their homes for use in Peyote meetings.

The legality of using peyote has been challenged a number of times because of the alleged dangerous effects of the drug. The first legal challenge came in 1899 when the agent for the Cheyenne and Arapaho asked that the state of Oklahoma ban the use of peyote; the state legislature ruled the drug illegal. Indians caught in possession of the drug were fined $25. However, after the famous Comanche Quanah Parker, a leader in the Peyote movement, testified before the state on behalf of his people that eating peyote was a necessary part of the ceremony, the law was repealed in 1908. While some states have barred the use of peyote, there has been no federal legislation because members of the Peyote cult incorporated as the Native American Church with a federal charter in 1918.

In 1960, a suit was filed against a Navajo for possession of peyote in Arizona. Judge Yale McFate ruled that since peyote was not a narcotic and was not habit forming, and, most of all, since the federal government in no way prohibited use of the drug, its usage as part of a religious practice could not be prohibited without interfering with a person's constitutional right to freedom of religion. While a number of states still have legislation preventing the transportation or use of peyote, the white man's law has in no way constricted the Native American Church.

Since peyote has caused so much controversy, yet remains an integral part of the religion of over a quarter-million Indians, it will be good to investigate more about the actual philosophy and rituals of the Native American Church. The fact that the church is incorporated makes it unique among Indian religions. In addition, the Native American Church incorporates a great deal of Christian doctrine along with native ritual. Thus Peyotism is what anthropologists call a syncretic religion, a religion influenced by more than one doctrine.

As in Christianity, there are sects. Peyotism has two: the Half Moon, by far the most popular, and the Cross Fire. The rituals of the two sects differ somewhat, the greatest distinction being that the Cross Fire sect uses the Bible in its ceremonies. In addition to having two sects, Peyote meetings are likely to vary in ceremony from one tribe to another, or even from one practitioner to another in one tribe. If all the members of the meeting are from the same tribe, the ceremony is usually held in the tribe's language. If members from different tribes attend the meeting, it is usually held in English, or each prays in his own tongue. Because of the many dissimilarities in practice, it would be difficult to describe all variations of Peyotism. But there are some customs, rituals, and paraphernalia that are common to all ceremonies.

Peyote meetings are held on Saturday nights, usually from sundown to sunup on Sunday. The ceremony takes place in a tepee which is especially set up for the occasion and dismantled after the meeting is concluded. The doorway of the tepee faces east. Inside, an altar is

built. There is a fireplace in the center of the lodge and
directly behind it a crescent-shaped altar made of earth.
On top of the altar is placed a large peyote button
called the father, or chief peyote. Between the fire and
altar is another crescent made from ashes. Between the
fireplace and doorway are placed food and water which
will later be ceremonially eaten and drunk.

The key members of the meeting are assigned special
seats inside the tepee. The Peyote chief, also called the
roadman, sits directly opposite the doorway in the rear
of the tepee, the traditional place of honor. On his right
sits the drum chief and on his left the cedar chief. Next
to the doorway sits the fire boy. The rest of the members sit around the inner perimeter of the tepee. If a
Bible is used, it is usually placed between the earth
altar and the Peyote chief.

Each member has his own ritual paraphernalia which
he stores and carries in a Peyote box, usually a long
rectangular box made of wood and decorated with
inlaid silver designs exclusive to the Native American
Church. These designs include representations of the
crescent moon, tepee, water turkey (a messenger of
God), star, and utensils used in the ceremony. The box
usually contains a loose fan, so called because the feathers are not stationary but rather hang freely from the
handle, each feather being attached to long rolled,
fringed ends; a large chief peyote; a staff, constructed
from three sections of wood and joined together by
means of inserted ferrels, which represents the staff of
life and also, symbolically, a bow with no strings (a
symbol of peace); and a gourd rattle which represents
an arrow. Most Peyotists wear a blanket made of red
and blue material, the red representing the day, the
blue the night.

The drum chief provides a Peyote drum made from a

three-legged brass kettle over which is stretched a hide. The kettle is partially filled with water to regulate the tone, and the hide is tied to the kettle by a rope in such a manner that, when completed, the rope forms an outline of the Morning Star on the underside of the drum.

Peyote meetings may be held for specific purposes: curing, birthday celebrations, funerals, memorials, for persons leaving the community to travel great distances, or for those returning from the armed services or school. Some are simply prayer meetings conducted on a regular schedule similar to Christian services. Usually, the persons wishing to participate in the ceremony arrive at the appointed home of the sponsor where the tepee has been erected. At dusk, the Peyote chief asks all who wish to take part to follow him into the tepee. He usually leads the line of members single file once around the outside of the tepee before they enter. Once inside, they take their appointed seats. When all are assembled the ritual paraphernalia is put in place.

The Peyote chief places the chief peyote upon the altar and the cedar chief sprinkles cedar needles on the central fire. Instead of using the traditional smoking pipe, cigarettes made from corn husk and tobacco are rolled and passed around the circle of participants. When the ritual smoking is ended, the ashes of the cigarettes are collected and placed near the altar. Sage is passed around, and each member rubs some of the sage on his body or chews a piece of it. Next the peyote buttons are passed out to each member who takes four buttons to begin. At this point the singing starts.

The Peyote chief takes some sage, the staff, and gourd rattle and tells the drum chief to begin drumming. As the drum resounds, the Peyote chief sings the opening song of the ceremony. This is a rather standardized song

In 1894 John K. Hillers photographed these three Indians (*left to right*): Big Looking Glass, a Comanche, holding a typical Peyote drum; Apache John, a Kiowa Apache, holding staff, gourd, and straight fan; and Apiatan, a Kiowa. (*Smithsonian Institution*)

at all Peyote meetings, no matter what tribe. He sings it four times, the sacred number of most Plains tribes. When he finishes, each member in turn eats some of the peyote buttons and sings four songs. The man on the right of the singer plays the drum while the singer shakes the gourd rattle. In this manner the ritual of eating and singing progresses around the tepee clockwise. The particularly fast drumming on the water drum and the rapid phrasing of the Peyote songs may have a great deal to do with creating the hallucinatory effects experienced in Peyote meetings. James H. Howard, a well-known anthropologist who has earned the right to lead Peyote meetings, believes that most of the sensory distortion of the participants is greatly influenced by the rapid drumming and constant staring into the fire, rather than by the effects of the drug itself.

Concurrent with the visionary experience is the feeling of a closeness with God. Because Peyotism is now greatly influenced by Christianity, the members pray to Jesus Christ and refer to the peyote as the Eucharist. They equate the consumption of the peyote button with Holy Communion and espouse the basic tenets of the Christian churches in their prayers and songs. The great difference between members of the Native American Church and those who would take peyote for kicks is that the avid Peyotists cannot understand how the sacred plant can be used for anything but prayer. To abuse the drug would be sacrilegious to Peyotists.

The praying, eating of peyote, and singing continue until midnight when there is a special ceremony. The fire boy informs the Peyote chief that it is midnight and then leaves the tepee to get a bucket of water. He returns with the water and presents it to the Peyote chief who dips a feather into the bucket and splashes water on the people in the tepee. After smoking and praying, the water is passed around to the members so that each may drink. During this part of the ceremony another standardized song is sung. After the midnight water drinking, the bucket is removed and it is time to resume the peyote eating and singing.

Before each major segment of the ritual, the cedar chief burns incense and the members purify themselves and their paraphernalia in the smoke. The ceremony lasts until dawn when a woman is called into the lodge bearing another bucket of water. She is called the morning water woman and is usually a relative of the Peyote chief, who now sings the dawn song. After praying and smoking again, the water is passed around the tepee. The Peyote chief smokes and prays and may doctor those who are ill, or simply pray for the welfare of the people. After the ceremonial water drinking, the woman retrieves the bucket and leaves the tepee. The Peyote chief then sings the "quittin' song" while the morning water woman goes for food which has been prepared for the traditional breakfast. The food consists of water, corn, fruit, and meat.

It is amazing to what degree the Native American Church has been influenced by Christianity and to what extent the native elements are translated in Christian terms. While there is no question that the Peyote ritual as it was originally practiced by the Aztec and neighboring tribes of Mexico was pure, virtually all Peyote rites nowadays are Christian in doctrine.

Silver earrings, brooches, and various other articles of costuming and clothing are popular among members of the Native American Church. Pins and earrings made from German silver in designs representative of Peyotism are worn with frequency by non-Peyotists also.

Although Peyotism is frowned on by many missionaries despite the Christian influence, the Native American Church thrives. It has already become increasingly popular among tribes who were once adherents of their native religion or outright Christians. In the early years Peyotism was extremely popular with adjacent communities of black Americans, and today many non-Indians are joining the Native American Church. While the controversy of its legality and morality is not likely to wane in view of increased use of drugs in general, the American Indian considers Peyote a valid form of religion not likely to be corrupted by prejudiced publicity or thrill-seeking whites.

9

Costumes and Crafts

ALTHOUGH the Plains Indians' attire has served as the stereotype for all forms of tribal dress, there was a time when distinctions between tribes could be determined by the style of clothing and methods of decoration and design. The stereotype is usually that of the Indian wearing a warbonnet, buckskin suit, and beaded moccasins. Only relatively few tribes inhabiting the United States ever actually dressed in this manner. Of those that did, there were other more prominent distinctions than are usually acknowledged.

At one time Indian art tended to be mostly functional. Not only clothing, but also dwellings, horse trappings, utensils, and games were heavily ornamented with painted designs, quillwork, beadwork, ribbon work, silver. As many Indian institutions disappeared, so did the need for their respective utensils, tools, and decorative techniques.

For example, when the Indian lived in tepees, first made of buffalo skins but later replaced by canvas, the tepees were decorated with painted designs on the cover and streamers from the lodge poles. So, too, were all the interior furnishings, such as willow backrests, cases for storage, cooking utensils, as well as personal objects. After the reservation period, Indians began living in frame houses, and slowly the tepee and all that was needed to maintain the house gave way to innovations of the white man. As the tepee way of life disappeared, there was no longer a need for its accessories. Modern cooking utensils replaced the old. Spring mattresses replaced the willow backrests and buffalo hide beds. As the automobile replaced the horse, the need for ornate saddle blankets, beaded martingales, and decorated bridles diminished. Although vestiges of the tepee and horse trappings are occasionally seen at Indian parades and events, the old ways of living and traveling have given way to modern times.

By the same token, however, those institutions which survive tend to encourage the continuation of Indian art. Among the Southern Plains tribes those arts which have survived are connected with Indian secular events, such as powwows in which hundreds of dancers replace the white man's clothing with feathers and beadwork.

The survival—and in the past twenty years a resurgence—of Indian singing and dancing (powwowing, as it is frequently called) and Peyotism has served to distinguish the Southern Plains Indians from their Northern neighbors. This distinction has been particularly noticeable in the costuming of the dancer since the beginning of World War I. Some styles of costuming have been undergoing changes similar to fashion trends while others have remained unchanged. In speaking of these styles we may discuss three general modes of costuming: old-time; feathers costume, also called fancy dance costume; and straight dance costume.

Old-time costumes usually refer to those which are

Hair Hanging Down, a Comanche, has leggings and shirt decorated with rolled fringe and holds a loose fan of eagle feathers.
He was photographed in Lawton, Oklahoma, by De Lancey Gill
in 1930. (*Smithsonian Institution*)

distinguishably tribal in nature. Thus an old-time Apache costume would differ drastically from an old-time Cheyenne costume. There would be less difference between Cheyenne and Arapaho, and Comanche and Kiowa. The old-time styles of dress are quickly dying and are noticeable only during parades or special tribal events.

As white men made contact with the Indians, articles of clothing usually made from natural resources such as deer, elk, and buffalo skin were slowly replaced by imported wools and cotton materials. Government-issued blankets replaced buffalo robes, and the convenience of European materials and sewing utensils made it easier for Indians to manufacture their clothing from the new goods. Thus the basic materials changed, but the Indians continued to decorate their everyday clothing with Indian designs. With the abundance of beads, ribbon, and other trade goods, plus an unusual amount of leisure time created by reservation living, there was an abundance of beadwork during the mid-nineteenth century. Ribbon appliqué work and German silver work were also in abundance. As more Indians turned toward the white man's road, the amount of native crafts diminished until approximately World War I. There was another decline after World War II, but since that time Indian craftwork is increasingly becoming important among the Southern Plains tribes.

From a resurgence of interest in Indian customs by Indian people themselves, a style of costuming evolved out of the World War I period (actually parts of the costuming can be traced to earlier periods) which has earned the name feathers, or fancy dance, costume because the costume is the uniform of the young Indian fancy dancer and is distinguishable by its two feather bustles worn on the rump and behind the neck in match-

A Caddo man and his horse photographed by James Mooney in 1893. The man's clothing is made from newly imported trade cloth which ultimately all but replaced fabric made from buckskin. (*Smithsonian Institution*)

ing pairs. The feathers costume knows no tribal boundaries; members of virtually all Southern Plains tribes, as well as members of tribes from other parts of the United States, have adopted the feathers costume as the official dress for powwows and dance contests.

The distinctive bustles are made in a variety of ways. The accepted and cherished feather is from the eagle, although other kinds of feathers are used nowadays since the killing of eagles is prohibited by federal law. The feathers are assembled to form a circle, a U-shape, or butterfly bustle, also known as a swing bustle because the feathers are arranged in such a manner that they swing freely as the Indian dances. The feathers are often prepared by adding hackle feathers of maribou to the base and tips, as well as colored dots and various other ornamental markings. The neck and back bustle match, making them a beautiful adjunct to any dancer's costume.

In addition to the elaborate bustle sets, the Oklahoma fancy dancers wear other articles of costuming which, though similar in construction, are different in ornamental style. The prized headdress is made from porcupine guard hair and deer tails. The hair is woven together and sewn to a base. The finished piece somewhat resembles the roached mane of a horse and is therefore referred to as a roach. Projecting from the middle of the roach are one or two eagle feathers which swivel in bone or metal sockets as the dancer moves about. Since roach making is a highly skilled art and very time consuming, many of them are imported and bought from Northern Plains tribes to help fulfill the demand. A long-haired roach sometimes reaching to the dancer's shoulders is one of the most valued pieces of the costume.

As basic clothing, the fancy dancer wears a pair of

swim trunks and usually a T-shirt, most often black. Over the swim trunks, he wears beaded aprons, a vestige of the breechcloth, composed of two pieces of cloth, one hanging in front, the other behind. Since the back apron is usually covered by the bustle, only the front apron is elaborately designed in beadwork. Moccasins made by the Cheyenne have always been considered ideal. The Cheyenne make their moccasins in such a way that they may be resoled when they wear out. Since moccasins are expensive, those which can last a long time are preferred. Around the ankles the dancers wear anklets made from finely combed Angora goat hair sometimes topped with a beaded strip. Bells are worn below the knee and buckled or tied on the inside of the leg so that the bells will not strike each other as the dancer moves or possibly lock.

To complete the costume, the dancers wear beaded cuffs, chokers, armbands, a wide belt, and galluses, or suspenders, sometimes called a harness. Ideally the beadwork and designs match on these items. Headbands are rather optional. Some dancers wear as a headdress a feathered crest resembling the general shape of the hair roach but made completely from stripped quills to which maribou has been attached. These headdresses, although not as popular as the hair roach, may be traced back to the turn of the century when there was a prototype headdress made of both hair and stripped quills.

While "war paint" is really a misnomer today, fancy dancers do paint their faces and bodies when they participate in Indian dances. Usually the dancers paint their arms and legs with zigzag or horizontal stripes. Face paint consists of the red witch paint across the eyes, or stripes across the cheeks. The painting has lost its significance, except as a method of decorating the uncostumed parts of the body.

The straight dance outfit is most often worn by members of the Pawnee, Osage, Oto-Missouri, and other lower-Siouan tribes. Just as the fancy dance costume is the uniform of the young war dancer, the straight dance costume identifies the more conservative dancers and is more closely related to the old-time style of dress, even though the straight dance outfit today transcends tribal boundaries. It is the costume of the dignified style associated with the original Hedushka Society. Not only the dance is traditional; so are the songs.

Just as the fancy dance costumes are similar in general style but individualistic in design, so is it true of the straight dance costume. It noticeably lacks the neck and back bustles of the fancy costume. Its outstanding characteristics are found in the elaborately colored shirts, matching cloth leggings, breechcloth, trailer, and abundance of otter skin accouterments.

Like the fancy dance costume, the traditional headdress of the straight dancer is the hair roach. However, one eagle feather serves to form the crest instead of two, reminiscent of the Pawnee "man standing in the fire." Many straight dancers wear an otter skin turban which was characteristically worn by many of the Prairie tribes in times long past. Often the turban is decorated with beaded rosettes. A single trailer of otter skin hangs from the back of the turban. The otter skin turban also is frequently won by the leaders of the Native American Church during the ceremonies.

When wearing a hair roach, the straight dancer may also wear two smaller eagle feathers—sometimes pheasant or magpie are substituted—called Hedushka feathers. These feathers are highly decorated with beadwork, hackle feathers, silver dangles, and sometimes exotic bird feathers such as parrot. They are attached to a cir-

cular disk sometimes beaded or made of silver and tied
to the dancer's hair or roach strings, and hang down in
front of the dancer's forehead. In addition to the roach
and Hedushka feathers, the dancer may optionally wear
a headband, usually a white handkerchief folded and
tied in front with a square knot.

According to individual taste, straight dancers wear a
variety of colored shirts made from silk or brocade.
They are collarless and hang loosely below the waist.
The cuffs and shoulder seams are decorated with ribbon work. Behind, roughly over each shoulder blade, is
a long silk scarf, one corner of which is filled with
sweetgrass, or a peyote button is tied to form a ball and
attached to the shirt. Around the neck the dancer wears
a silk or brocade scarf held in place by a silver necker-
chief slide. Around his throat he wears a beaded or
bone choker. Over each shoulder, crossing in front and
behind, is a pair of bandoliers, usually made from
aurora borealis beads, and bone hair pipes, or tubular
bones tapered at each end. Silver armbands are worn,
but there are no beaded cuffs.

The breechcloth, trailer, and leggings of the straight
dancer are made from a wool material called trade
cloth, which has a rainbow selvaged edge. They are
decorated with fine ribbon-work appliqué and beadwork edging. The leggings are worn in such a way that
the seam overlaps at the front of the leg. They are tied
below the knee with woven garters over which are
buckled two or three rows of bells. The garters match a
woven sash which is worn around the waist but under
the shirt. The ends of the sash hang below the shirt at
the sides. A wide loomed, beaded belt is worn over the
shirt. The breechcloth is tucked between the legs, hanging in front and behind. An additional trailer hangs
from behind, nearly reaching the ground. An otter tail

trailer, or drop, hangs from the dancer's neck between his shoulders, also almost reaching the ground. The otter tail trailer is usually decorated with beaded rosettes. To finish the costume, the dancer wears a pair of partially or fully beaded moccasins. He traditionally carries a feather fan, and upon special occasions, if he has been so honored because of his proficiency, a small cane decorated with fine beadwork, fur, and sometimes feathers.

This item-by-item description of the fancy dance and straight dance costumes is intended to point out a few things of importance.

First, most people are not aware of the details that go into making a costume. Even though we can draw a distinction between fancy and straight costumes, imagine the number of variations possible within each category based on individual taste—such as materials, designs, optional items. Certainly by comparing just these two styles of costume, we see that there is no such thing as *an* Indian costume. If we were to examine the classical tribal styles, this would be even more evident.

Secondly, a great amount of time and money must go into assembling such costumes. In the straight dance costume alone there are approximately twenty items which make up the complete costume. Each item takes a great deal of time to make, and all the items are costly. A good hair roach, for instance, may cost as much as a hundred dollars. Prices of all raw materials and finished goods have tended to be higher in Oklahoma than on the Northern Plains—chiefly because some Oklahoma tribes have been able to afford quality materials. But the time and money involved also indicate the Indian's appreciation of his own culture. To the Indian, the articles of costuming which represent his culture are worth it. They have a value that transcends dollar value. Often the accumulation of these things means a great sacrifice to the Indian, yet he gladly makes the sacrifice.

It is not only in costume, the emblem of social events, that the Indian applies time, money, and craft. As pointed out before, a great deal of craftsmanship is involved in preparing certain ritual objects used in the Native American Church.

Although trading posts which cater to the tourist trade are abundant on the Southern Plains, the Indian craftsman does not primarily earn his income from objects sold to non-Indians. While a few collectors are willing to pay any price for objects to which they take a fancy, the average tourist is satisfied with a piece of Hong Kong beadwork as a memento of his trip to Indian country. Most craft articles are made *by* Indians *for* Indians, and in many cases the transaction is made by barter rather than money. Many articles are simply given by one Indian to another as a token of esteem, a custom which has survived among the Indian peoples.

That Indian art has survived at all will probably come as a surprise, for as certain institutions die, there is no longer need for certain kinds of crafts. True, many craft techniques have been consigned to the display cases of museums, but others, as in the case of the Native American Church, are replacing older institutions. Also, though American Indians today dress like others in their geographic region, there is a tendency for Indians to dress up Indian style outside the realm of ceremonials.

For example, many articles of costuming are actually worn as dress-up clothing at either Indian or non-Indian events. The ten-gallon hat usually sports a beaded headband. Many Indian men wear beaded Indian bolo ties and belts even at non-Indian occasions.

An Oto, Who Makes a Noise While Walking, wears an otter fur turban, ball, and cone trade earrings, besides a bear claw necklace. Taken around 1880. *(Smithsonian Institution)*

At some secular events, men may also wear the red and blue Peyote blankets and beaded moccasins. Women seem to be more traditional than men. In addition to the buckskin dresses and cloth dresses they wear at powwows, Indian women can be found wearing Peyote jewelry and the traditional shawls as part of their everyday clothing.

The Southern Plains Indian truly recognizes the value of those crafts that are irrefutably Indian. Indians living in Oklahoma have been pointed out by experts for their extreme accent on quality in raw materials and finished products. Their costumes are often described as "finely tailored." Although even the finest craftsman cannot truly make a full-time living in producing his handiwork, the idea of craftsmanship as an identifying force in Indian culture will remain as valid in years to come as it was in the past.

10

Music and Dance

TODAY, as well as in times gone by, music and dance are an integral part of the Indian way of life. Virtually no part of religious or purely social life of the Indian is possible without music and dance. Though prayers were offered up to the deities in spoken language, those prayers that were sung were considered to be more potent, more pleasing, to the Great Spirit.

The dramatic highlights of all religious convocations were acted out in ritual song and dance. From the moment a warrior was born till the time he died, songs were sung about his great exploits. When he returned from a successful hunt or foray against the tribal enemies, he acted out his adventures in dance drama so that all the people of the tribe could witness his achievements. The history and traditions of the people were partially recorded in songs; the strength and virility of warriors recorded in their dance movements.

Since all aspects of American Indian life have been misinterpreted and stereotyped, it is no wonder early travelers reported that Indian music was loud and fierce, with shrieking resembling the cries of wild animals, and that their dancing was uncontrolled jumping and hopping about in a frenzy of savage primitivism. Not until the latter part of the nineteenth century did students of American Indian music and dance begin to note the subtleties and great varieties of music and dance. The fallacy that all Indian music sounds alike was dispelled by such experts as Alice C. Fletcher and Frances Densmore, two of the earliest recorders and interpreters of Indian music.

Once American Indian music and dance were identified as true art forms, there was another period—a period we might refer to as the romantic period—in which a number of books were written for young people to teach them the Indian music and dance. Unfortunately, as in the case of most romanticists, the authors' descriptions of songs and dances were mostly figments of their imaginations. True, many of the dances were based on original Indian dances and themes, but somewhere their authenticity was lost in the translation. In some cases, many sacred dances which were and still are considered parts of religious ceremonies were described for the purpose of teaching young non-Indians how to perform them for shows.

Today we are living in a more realistic age. Those who wish to learn music and dance travel to the reservations and various Indian communities to learn at first hand. In this regard, Oklahoma and the Southern Plains Indians have played an unusually important part in disseminating music and dance styles. Oklahoma style, as it is often called, has become largely accepted in many parts of the country as *the* Indian style of music and dance. Just what constitutes Oklahoma style is an interesting study in itself since it represents a fusion of many styles with emphasis on what was originally of the

Plains. To the Plains elements of music and dance have been added styles from other cultural areas.

Before the establishment of Indian Territory and the ultimate removal of Indian tribes to a highly concentrated area—Oklahoma—music and dance were identifiable to a large degree by tribe. Tribal styles differed; music which contained words was sung in the native language of each respective tribe. Historically, many elements of music and dance had passed from one tribe to another even before the removal to Indian Territory. Once removed to Oklahoma, however, the borrowing of ideas intertribally rapidly accelerated. Indians speaking different languages and observing different traditions now lived close together. They were able to visit each other, and soon, out of this concentration of tribes, there arose a number of song types and dances which could be enjoyed by members of all tribes. Although the songs and dances mutually acceptable by all tribes had their source in tribal or non-Indian origin, the music and dance styles soon began to be identified as what anthropologists call Pan-Indian. Later we shall discuss this term more completely as it is sometimes used indiscreetly and leads one to believe that the Indians are becoming one big All-American tribe.

Thus intertribal music and dance are relatively easy to identify and discuss because the music and dance are very vital to Indians today. There are relatively few kinds of dances, but there are many songs which may be sung for these dances. While each song and dance can be historically traced to tribal roots, much of the tradition of music and dance has been rather neglected, except by a handful of scholars, Indian and non-Indian.

The most popular dance on the Southern Plains is commonly called the war dance, today purely a social function. It is a dance primarily for men, though

A young Kiowa-Apache woman wearing buckskin dress and boots. (*Smithsonian Institution*)

women participate to a lesser degree. The war dance is one in which the dancer may show off his individual style. He performs a number of intricate steps in time to the drumming and singing that are provided by a number of singers who seat themselves around a large dance drum which they beat with drumsticks. One man leads the songs while the group, including female singers, joins in each chorus. The dancers, although performing individual dance movements, dance in a group in a clockwise direction around the center of a dance area.

There are basically two forms of war dance—fancy dance and straight dance. The dancers wear costumes corresponding to those described in the previous chapter. The term "fancy dance" comes from the fact that the dancers use intricate steps and body movements. It is primarily used for dance contests, which have become increasingly popular since the turn of the century. The straight dance is more conservative and resembles the older form of traditional dancing. During the course of a normal powwow, most dance straight, although some may at times cut loose into fancy steps, dipping quickly, doing fast spins, and tapping one foot in front and behind the other.

Most war dance songs are sung in vocables, or meaningless syllables, that serve to carry the tune of the song. While each war dance song is different, their structures are the same. Thus the dancers can stop on the last beat of the drum, even though they have never heard the song before. This is considered especially important as a characteristic of good Oklahoma war dancing.

Not all but a good number of straight dance songs are sung with words reminiscent of old tribal battles. As mentioned earlier, the Ponca are considered to be the foremost exponents of the straight dance song and are invited to sing for many of the older traditional straight dances.

Both the fancy and straight war dances are vestiges of the older Hedushka dance. The straight dance is still called by that name among the Ponca. Variations of the word (Irushka, Helushka) are also used by other tribes when speaking their own language.

Women participate in the war dances to a lesser degree. They dance in a rather reserved walking step in the same direction as the men. During the middle of each war dance song, there are loudly accented beats called honor beats. During this part of the song the women dance toward the drum located in the center of the dance area and dip slowly, as if slightly bowing. This is called honoring the drum and is important for women to perform during the course of a dance.

Next in importance is the round dance. The name comes from its obvious formation: Dancers, both men and women, sidestep clockwise forming a circle as they dance. Most experts agree that the round dance was originally done as a women's scalp dance. In times past, it was customary among many Plains tribes for the women to carry the battle gear of their male relatives, including scalps they had taken, in a victory celebration. The women, carrying scalps suspended from poles, danced in a circle while the singers described the exploits of the returning warriors.

Today the round dance usually starts off the pow-wows. The music, also provided by a chorus of singers, is some of the most beautiful on the Southern Plains. Because no particular kind of costume is needed to perform the round dance, men, women, and children, including non-Indian visitors, are often asked to participate. One of the relatively recent innovations in the round dance is a kind of Indian square dance. The

Dog Chief, also known as Simond Adams, a Pawnee, taken around 1929. He wears an old-time straight dance costume. He has a beaded cane and an especially wide beaded strip on his blanket. (*Smithsonian Institution*)

dancers begin by doing the round dance but then go into a number of patterns resembling a Virginia reel, complete with swing your partner and forming bridges under which the couples dance. Today the round dance is performed all over the United States and has come to be equated with a kind of national Indian dance indicative of friendship of all Indian peoples.

Another circle dance which has been especially popular in Oklahoma among the young people is called the forty-nine. The name of this dance has been the object of great discussion over a number of years. At one time there was a popular theory that the name came from the fact that 50 warriors went on the warpath and only one returned, and so the dance was created to honor the 49 who had been killed. The story also appeared in reverse, that is, 50 left and 49 returned and the dance was performed for the 49 who returned safely.

While both make interesting stories, the more probable origin was described by Norman Feder, curator of American Indian art at the Denver Art Museum, who has spent a great deal of time studying Indians of the Southern Plains. According to Feder, the name forty-nine likely comes from an incident in which some young Indians who had been excessively drinking wanted to attend a sideshow at a local carnival but didn't have the money. The sideshow was called something like "Days of '49." Because the Indians were drunk and penniless, they were not admitted to the show. One allegedly said, "Let's go have our own '49," and proceeded to sing and dance in a secluded spot using a washtub for a drum.

The forty-nine is still danced in secluded areas. The singers stand in the center of the area, most often using a tub or cardboard box as a drum. They sing songs which can be traced to old Kiowa war journey songs, though today the newer songs are purely social in nature and rarely contain words. Those that do sometimes employ English words. One of the most popular goes: "I don't care if you marry sixteen times. I love you, I'll get you yet!"

Another, sometimes called the "Mae West Song," simply says: "Why don't you come up and see me sometime?"

The dancers form a number of concentric circles tightly about the singers, young men and women locking arms. The singers start off the song and the dancers join in the choruses. They dance with a simple walking step to the side in a clockwise direction.

Forty-nines are always held at nighttime and sometimes last until sunup. They usually begin after the regular powwow has finished. Because drinking and fighting sometimes result, many non-Indians frown upon forty-nines. When a drum is used, they claim that the sound carries for miles and keeps them awake. Consequently, the forty-nines are often disbanded by local police.

Once in full swing, however, forty-nines are not easy to break up. After being chased from one dance area, the young people jump in their cars and head for another secluded spot. Thus the chase may go on all night. Today, especially in urban areas, forty-nines are sometimes danced indoors, but some of the charm is lost when it is removed from its natural environs.

One particularly exciting dance, which has been borrowed by the Plains tribes from the Southeast, is the stomp dance. Originally, the stomp dance was performed as a ceremony by the Five Civilized Tribes (it still is today by those tribes). But after the Plains tribes learned it, the dance lost its ceremonial significance and became purely social.

Like the forty-nine, costumes are not required for the stomp dance. It is a follow-the-leader, serpentine dance in which men and women participate. Often a stomp dance is performed concurrently with a forty-nine, the young dancers leaving one to participate in the other held a few yards away.

No drum is used. Instead, several young women called shakers wear several turtleshells or, in recent times, tin can rattles strapped to each leg. To prevent being cut from the cans or the wires that hold them together, the women wear a protective covering of cloth under the rattles. The leader is a young man who knows all the stomp dance songs. A shaker takes her place behind the leader, and behind her, another young man who also knows the songs. Ideally, the dancers alternate in the line, a woman behind each man.

The songs are of the call-and-answer variety. The leader calls out a short phrase and the rest of the dancers respond as they follow him, stomping about the dance grounds. Although originally the calls and answers had words, for the most part only meaningless syllables are used. Like the forty-nine, occasional English phrases are inserted into the song. For instance, the leader sings: "Listen to me, honey, I got the blues." The dancers respond in vocables: "Wah-hee-yoh-wah-hee-yay." The leader continues: "I got the blues and I gottem over you." And again the dancers repeat: "Wah-hee-yoh-wah-hee-yay."

There are a great number of calls and answers, and the good leaders are chosen based on their repertory and leading style. Some of the leaders have their own idiosyncrasies. Some may cup their hands over their mouths so that the call is loud and clear. Others wear big ten-gallon hats and occasionally wave them over their heads while they are dancing. Often the leader is forced into leading a stomp. As the young man enters the dance area he is quickly recognized by the other dancers who immediately line up behind him. Whether he is in the mood to lead or not, the rest of the dancers insist by following him around the dance area until he begins the first call.

The music of the stomp dance is particularly pleasing, even to those who have never heard Indian music. The melodies are reminiscent of Negro blues, and some leaders effect a slight yodel in their voice when they sing. The chorus is more greatly enhanced by the montonous chik-chik, chik-chik of the shakers. While the dance is often a simple follow-the-leader dance, sometimes the leader wraps up the group by dancing in a small circle until all the dancers are intertwined in the middle of the circle. At a given signal by the leader, they reverse and unwind themselves.

Another dance, partly indigenous to the Plains and partly imported from the Southwest, is the snake and buffalo dance. While actually two separate dances, they are always performed together, one after the other. The snake dance, which comes from the Southwest (but should not be confused with the famous Hopi snake dance in which live rattlesnakes are used) is performed in a line. One man serves as the head of the snake, another as the tail. As the dance progresses the leader gives a signal and all dancers turn around and follow the tail. At the conclusion of the snake dance the dancers spread out on the dance area and begin the buffalo dance. During the buffalo dance, the dancers imitate the actions of the buffalo milling about and

then, in time with the jump, begin doing short hops
supposedly imitating a bird that lived among the
buffalo herds.

There are other specials, such as the Indian two-step,
a partner dance for men and women, and a number of
show dances, such as the spear and shield dance in
which two warriors simulate enemies fighting, and the
hoop dance, in which a soloist shows his ability to
manipulate a hoop over and around his body.

All of these constitute the principal dances performed
by the Southern Plains Indians today. They are an integral part of every Oklahoma powwow and are also
popular in urban areas where a large number of Indians
have relocated. In addition, there are a number of songs
and dances which are not as universal as those mentioned. Although Oklahoma is known for its intertribal
dances, there are a multitude of songs and dances which
are decidedly tribal in nature. The Kiowa, for example,
in their Black Legging Society and Gourd Dance Clan
have their own songs and dances which are not shared
by other tribes. At strictly Kiowa events, the societies
are active in sponsoring the dances and performing the
older forms of song and dance.

One unusual presentation made by the Gourd Dance
Clan is the use of a military bugler in one of their
dances. It is said that long ago the members of the
Gourd Dance Clan captured a U.S. bugler and forced
him to sound the charge as they celebrated their victory.
Traditionally, it became a high honor to try to count
coup on a bugler or capture him and bring him back to
the Kiowa encampment. To this day, the commandant
at Fort Sill, Oklahoma, provides a regular Army bugler
to sound the charge while the Gourd Clan members are
performing their clan songs and dances in memory of

the time when the Kiowa warred against the United States troops.

A number of tribes still remember many old songs that are now no longer in use. The Cheyenne, Arapaho, Caddo, and other tribes that once participated in the ghost dance can still sing the songs, even though the ghost dance is no longer performed. Old songs such as these are particularly revered by the old people. They represent to them a life that will never return. On the other hand, this does not mean that Indian music and dance are by any means dying. They are only taking on new forms. Just as in the old days, certain men are known as fine singers and composers and continue to uphold the musical traditions of their people.

There is, for example, a song of relatively recent origin known by the Oklahoma tribes as the flag song. It is sung universally throughout the Southern Plains as an honoring song for the United States and essentially is interchangeable with the national anthem. The flag song may be sung without words, or in the native language of the various tribes. Since many Indians from Oklahoma served in the Forty-fifth Division of the U.S. Army, there is another special song sung at Indian events in honor of those Indian soldiers, and it is called the "Forty-fifth Division" or "Thunderbird" (the nickname of the division). It too may be sung with or without words. Thus Indian music is as vital today as before the white man came. Only the reasons for singing have changed.

In the Southern Plains the sun dance and ghost dance songs have largely been replaced by Peyote songs, which are composed every day. The songs once sung for warriors who fought against tribal enemies have been replaced by songs that extol the prowess of Indians who

fought against the enemies of the United States during
World Wars I and II, Korea, and Vietnam.

Dancers "dancing the drum" at Pawhuska in 1969. (*Photo by
S. Rhoades*)

11

Powwow Fever

THE DEGREE to which today's American Indian sings and dances may be summed up in a word—powwow! Of Algonquian derivation, the word *pauau* originally meant "curing ceremony." The first white men to witness this religious practice saw the great number of people in attendance and later erroneously coined the word to mean any gathering of Indian people.

Today Indians use the word "powwow" to signify a general gathering in which the primary emphasis is on singing, dancing, feasting, and the giving of gifts. The powwow is one of the major outlets through which the American Indian expresses his identity. During the summer months many Indian communities are hit with an almost uncontrollable disease of the spirit—powwow fever.

But the disease is benign because powwow fever infers having a good time, seeing old friends, and—at least temporarily—being Indian and following the Indian way of life. It means traveling superhighways and rutted roads—any thoroughfare that leads to the pounding of drums and the chorus of voices that invite all to sing, dance, and be Indian.

Although powwows may be held at any time, summer is when each tribe serves as host at a powwow to which members of other tribes are invited. There is a powwow being held virtually every weekend in the summertime. If time permits, you may travel the powwow circuit, going from one dance to the next with barely enough time to catch your breath.

One of the most important Indian events in the state of Oklahoma draws Indian as well as non-Indian spectators from all over the country. Officially called the American Indian Exposition, it is known locally to the Indians as the Fair. Each year thousands of Indians flock to Anadarko, Oklahoma, the "Indian capital of the nation," to take part in the week-long panorama of pageants, contests, craft exhibits, horse races, and carnival.

Located sixty miles southwest of Oklahoma City, Anadarko is the agency for the Kiowa, Comanche, and Apache tribes, and is rich in Western history. In 1931 the first exposition was held. It achieved fame as being the only Indian exposition of its kind to be completely run by an all-Indian committee made up of members of the Comanche, Kiowa, Caddo, Kiowa Apache, Osage, Cheyenne, Arapaho, Pawnee, Wichita, Oto-Missouri, Delaware, and Seminole.

In addition to local tribes, many others are invited to participate in the exposition. Beginning with a colorful parade through Anadarko on the first day, each day and night is taken up by a host of Indian demonstrations of tribal dancing, crafts, archery contests, horse races, and pageants. Those who come from afar pitch their tents and tepees on the edge of town near the pageant grounds. In addition to tents, many families build willow arbors and cook shades.

The days and nights are occupied with visiting friends in camp and preparing for the evening's activities. The exposition committee hires over two hundred Indians to participate in the afternoon activities and dance each night. The daylight events are highlighted by all-Indian band concerts, specialty dances, various Indian games of skill, such as the Creek stickball game—a game with very few rules other than getting the ball across the opponent's goal line, and one which has all the excitement of football, soccer, lacrosse, and hockey, with plenty of bruises. In the evening the pageant, written by Indians, is performed on alternate nights. Between pageant nights the tribes put on demonstrations of tribal dances. Traditionally on Friday night the national war dance championship is held. This is a major event in which individuals compete for high honors in dancing. For the women there is a contest for those wearing buckskin dresses and another for those wearing cloth dresses. For the men there are straight dance contests. The highlight of the evening is the men's junior and senior fancy dance contests.

I first attended the Indian Fair in 1952 after having spent some time earlier among various Indian communities in Oklahoma. Although I made subsequent trips to the fair, I can never forget my first impressions. The fairgrounds were located two miles south of Anadarko. By the time I arrived in town the people were already beginning to set up their camps on the grounds adjacent to the dance arena, even though the fair was not to begin for a few days. The Osage tents made of striped canvas, pale orange or green and white, stood out in contrast to the weather-worn gray tents of the other

Interior of an Osage dance house at Pawhuska, Oklahoma, in 1903. *(Museum of the American Indian, Heye Foundation)*

tribes. Some of the early arrivals took great pains in constructing tremendous willow shades, some measuring almost twenty-five feet in length, fashioned on an elliptical base typical of the Southern Plains tribes. The shades served as protection from the unbearably hot Oklahoma sun and also as eating and sleeping compartments for guests. Some smaller shades were used for cooking only.

A few tepees were scattered around the camp. The oldest woman of the Comanche family, with whom I stayed, insisted on erecting a tepee and made it open to anyone who needed a bed for the night. Despite her age, she, along with her family, set to the task of raising the tepee near the center of the campgrounds. Since attending the fair was a traditional annual affair, she, like each family, had earmarked a certain section of the campgrounds to put up her tent and shade. There was a tendency for members of the same tribe to camp near one another, though it was not a strict rule.

The elderly lady was remarkable. She was a traditional Comanche who spoke very little English. I was particularly impressed by her fastidiousness. She spent her free time cleaning up the area, keeping it free of debris by devising a simple underground disposal area, a neat square of earth which she dug up after carefully removing the sod. Any refuse was quickly disposed of in the hole and the sod put back as a lid to the earthen container to conceal the waste from view. When all her chores were finished, she kept a watchful eye over her grandchildren as she sat quietly in her shade doing beadwork.

More tents and shades were raised until, by the time the fair was to begin, there was scarcely room to walk. Children were constantly being admonished by their elders for knocking down the tent guidelines. Drivers were cautioned as they entered the road which encircled the camp area to drive carefully and watch for the bands of tots who scampered around the camp.

By the day before the fair was to begin almost ten thousand Indians had arrived at the campgrounds and more would be coming during the ensuing week.

On the first day the parade was held on the main street of Anadarko. The whole town turned out to watch the representatives of the tribes pass in review. All were dressed in tribal attire, some dancing and singing as they paraded through town. Each tribe had selected a young woman to represent her tribe as tribal princess. One would later be chosen as the official princess of the American Indian Exposition.

The fairgrounds were crowded with many tourists who sat in the stands to watch the horse racing and games. One section of the track had been set aside as the pageant and dance grounds. These were only temporary grounds for the activities. The Indians of the area had planned to build their own stadium which was partially under construction. The then-president, a Kiowa, Robert Goombi, along with a number of tribal princesses, had recently appeared on the Arthur Godfrey television show to help raise money to build their own exposition grounds. An organization had been incorporated under the name of the Redman Foundation, and people all over the country were asked to purchase two inches of Indian land for one dollar in order to raise the necessary money to complete the arena. Thousands responded. Their deeds to the land were actually recorded in the Caddo County Courthouse, and subsequently a new amphitheater was built to accommodate the pageant and ceremonial dances.

Next to the fairgrounds a local carnival was in full swing. The smell of sawdust, cotton candy, and the grinding of gears on the ferris wheel were noticeably out of place compared with the smell of burning wood and sounds of drums, bells, and singing voices of the Indians nearby. Yet the carnival had always been a main attraction of the fair and continues to be at many large Indian events throughout the country.

On the opposite side of the fairgrounds was a large building which housed an elaborate arts and crafts exhibit. Beadwork, featherwork, both modern and traditional crafts, were on display. They would later be judged by a panel of distinguished Indian judges and the craftsmen awarded ribbons for the best examples of arts and crafts. The exhibition hall not only served as a museum of fine Indian handicraft, but many of the local craftsmen sold items to visitors. Fine art work by the leading artists of the area was also on display.

The largest crowd gathered on the weekend. Friday night was the highlight—as far as the Indians were concerned—with the championship war dance contest. Young men from many of the tribes waited for this event with great anticipation, for to win this contest was a major achievement for any Indian dancer. The grandstand was crowded with Indians cheering for their favorite dancers. Although by non-Indian standards dancing is not normally considered an athletic achievement, Indian war dancing takes a great deal of stamina and strength coupled with artistry and poise. The individual movements of the war dancer are certainly an awesome sight even to the newcomer to Indian country.

Each of the contestants wore a large number on his front apron so that he could be readily identified by the audience and judges. The judges were made up of members of the fair committee, some of whom had been champion dancers in their younger days. The dancers

A junior fancy dance at Anadarko in 1970. Number 41, a girl Osage, pictured above, won first place. (*Photo by T. Stewart*)

were asked to line up in front of the dance area where they could be well viewed by judges and spectators. The singers seated around a large drum were signaled to start a song and give the dancers a warm-up. Some of the dancers began immediately with fancy steps, while others, saving their energy for the actual contest, held back.

War dance contests as well as other Indian dancing may be seen from two viewpoints. The white man views the whole event as a flashy blur of feathers dancing around without much rhyme but a lot of rhythm; but the Indian viewing the same dancers is looking for specific movements and style. Subtleties which often escape the tourist are often those very points which determine the winner of the contest. Judging, though considered an honor, is a difficult job with few or no rewards. The winner is always congratulated by the losers with warm handshakes and pats on the back.

The biggest difficulty in judging these contests is that there are few standards against which the dancers compete. The only hard and fast rules are that a dancer must keep in time with the singing and drumming, end on precisely the last beat of the drum, and, finally, make sure that his feathers are securely tied on. If an article of costuming falls off during the actual contest, he is automatically disqualified.

When the dancers and singers were ready, the head judge gave the signal and the great drum began to boom in the fast, steady beats of the war dance song. Immediately the dancers sprang into action, each performing his best and fanciest steps. They moved from side to side, in small circles, bobbing up and down. Their feet moved so rapidly one could hardly follow them. Their entire bodies danced, feathers swaying up and down, back and forth, in time to the rhythm of the singers. As the second song began, the drum boomed even louder, and the dancers seemingly obeying the commands of the drum by moving even more frenetically. Still dancing within the small space allocated them, but moving in even more indefinable steps, they darted quickly, crouching and then straightening their bodies again to full stature. The dancers sensed the final cadences of the song and began their trickiest steps. One dancer, an Oto-Missouri who had been the favorite of the evening, upon anticipating the last few beats of the song, suddenly turned a complete flip in the air. He ended his acrobatic feat on precisely the last beat of the song. The contest was over.

The judges were busily scribbling the numbers of their favorites on pads of paper while the dancers, breathing heavily, waited. The third-place winner was then announced as a young Comanche boy. The crowd responded with great applause while the singers hit the drum in acknowledgment of the winner. Next the second-place winner's name was called, a Kiowa. Again the audience and singers responded. Finally, after a short deliberation, the name of the young Oto-Missouri was announced and the crowd cheered while the other contestants rushed over to congratulate him. Each received an appropriate ribbon and cash prize, then was asked to dance a short song for the audience. Despite being tired from their recent ordeal, the young winners leaped into action as soon as the drum was struck and danced in rare form. The winners would retain the title until the following year when the war dance championships would be held again.

After the war dance championship had ended, there were a few more tribal dances before the program was concluded. The spectators left the stands and wandered about the fairgrounds. But for the Indians assembled, the dancing was not over. Changing out of their Indian costumes, they reassembled to dance the forty-nine.

The singers finally arrived. They had been unable to find a drum, so they carried a cardboard box upon which to beat. Parading to the center of the dance circle, just out of the glare of a spotlight, they began to hit the box with their drumsticks and sing favorite forty-nine songs. The young people quickly scampered, the first to arrive forming a circle around the singers. As more arrived they formed additional circles until finally there were no less than seven concentric circles of dancers moving around the singers. They danced slowly, stepping from side to side as they moved clockwise around the singers and their makeshift drum. As each chorus started the dancers would join in, all singing their favorite songs: "I got drunk on Porter Hill, sobered up in the Washita."

They laughed at the English lyrics. Around and around they danced, bobbing side to side in time to the songs: "I don't care if you marry sixteen times. I still love you, I'll get you yet."

After a while a young Quapaw man wearing a large black ten-gallon hat, with an eagle feather stuck in the band, appeared. From somewhere in the shadows came the heavy footsteps of young women wearing shakers around their legs. The young Quapaw was well known as a favorite stomp dance leader.

The young Quapaw entered the dance area next to the spot where the forty-niners were in full swing. Pretending not to notice anyone, he walked nonchalantly among his friends. Soon the shakers arrived and stood impatiently on the sidelines. The stomp dance leader seemed to be simply meandering around, looking for friends, but soon a young girl with shakers on stepped quickly behind him and followed him as he walked about. Soon another young man—the leader's second—moved in behind the shaker, and a second shaker quickly moved behind him. The stomp line was beginning to form, and other spectators began to join in. Still the leader walked around, looking for friends as if nobody were behind him. The forty-niners still continued to dance and sing oblivious of the new group forming next to them. Someone had arrived with a drum and the cardboard box was discarded. The dance area boomed.

Then the young Quapaw cupped a hand over his mouth and cried, "Hiyu-woooooo!" . . . the signal for the stomp dance to begin. Those behind him responded, "Hiyu-woooooo! . . ." The signal attracted young people who dashed to get in line behind the leader and shakers.

The song continued in short rhythmic calls and responses between leader and chorus. Soon the shakers began stepping, emphatically jarring their heels on the ground to make the shakers resonate. Chik-chik, chik-chik, the shakers resounded as they followed the leader in a serpentine movement around the area. Soon the voices of the stomp dancers and the forty-niners clashed. Some of the forty-niners left their circles to join in the stomp. The stomp dance line grew longer and longer until those at the tail had to run at almost full speed to keep up with those ahead of them. As they tired, they dropped out of the line and went over to the forty-nine, which continued as if nothing else were happening in the arena.

And so the young people danced for hours, moving back and forth from stomp line to forty-nine. As each stomp leader tired he was replaced by another.

Suddenly the dance was disrupted by a police siren and a revolving light that sped into the dance area. Two state troopers jumped out of the car and ordered the Indians to stop dancing. Townspeople from nearby Anadarko were complaining that the drum and voices were keeping them awake. As if by cue, the dancing stopped and the singers and dancers quickly moved out of the arena back to the campgrounds. This had been a familiar interruption in the past. They were prepared for it.

Soon they would be crammed into automobiles heading for a new dance site—Hill X or Snake Pit, two remote places near town. They would be chased again. But, moving from one remote place to another, the young people would continue their forty-nines and stomp dances until the rising sun told them it was time to return to camp.

So it has been each year at the fair. But Anadarko is not the only center of activities. When summer comes, virtually every Indian community becomes a dance ground. Even metropolitan areas such as Tulsa and Oklahoma City have become centers of Indian powwow activity.

One of the best-organized and well-attended powwows is the Pawnee Homecoming Powwow held each year over the July Fourth weekend. Dancers from all over the Southern Plains area assemble near Pawnee, Oklahoma, where an elaborate campground is set up. Participants are given food rations every day by the tribal committee. The powwow grounds have the atmosphere of an old-time celebration with much gift giving —especially to people who have traveled long distances to attend.

Other powwows are held throughout the state— Kiowa Gourd Dance Clan Powwow at Carnegie; Quapaw Indian Powwow at Quapaw; Ponca Indian Powwow at White Eagle; Cheyenne and Arapaho Powwow at Clinton; Osage Straight Dances at Hominy, Gray Horse, and Pawhuska. Intertribal powwows are held monthly in Tulsa and Oklahoma City, drawing well-known war dancers who compete for big cash prizes ranging as high as a thousand dollars for first prize.

But powwow fever is not limited to the state of Oklahoma alone. Other powwows are held in neighboring Kansas and Nebraska, as well as in urban areas of Texas. The small Omaha tribe holds an annual affair in Macy, Nebraska, and a large celebration in Mayetta, Kansas. In 1970, the Wichita Centennial Celebration featured a Mid-America All-Indian Days program in which Wichita, Osage, Comanche, Kiowa, Cheyenne, and Arapaho participated. Powwows have become so popular that they literally are the American Indian pastime. Virtually all tribes living on the Southern Plains, whether they are indigenous to the area or new-comers, sponsor some kind of Indian doings all year round. What was once considered only a tourist attraction is nowadays strictly for the Indian's enjoyment—tourists or not.

The overall effect of the powwow is to hold the members of many Indian nations together in a singular cohesiveness that is irrefutably Indian. Singing, dancing, and putting on one's feathers are a sign that the Indian spirit is far from dead. Only in outdated history books has the Indian physically or spiritually vanished.

12

Language

MORE THAN three thousand languages are spoken in the world today. For years many of them were classified as preliterate because they could not be written. But today scholars consider some languages more comprehensive than others because they express a number of concepts brought about mainly through technological change. In other words, as technology grew, more words were needed to express these new ideas.

For example, astronauts, while speaking English, have developed a verbal shorthand that is intelligible for the most part only to technicians of space travel. As their special language filters out to nontechnicians, some of the vocabulary becomes a part of everyday speech of the layman.

American Indian languages fall into the category of preliterate languages. Since the arrival of the white man, however, alphabets have been developed for many Indian languages; in some areas signs, newspapers, and books are available in native dialects. These alphabets were in the main developed first by missionaries who translated religious teachings into the tribal languages. Later linguists became interested in American Indian languages and took over where the missionaries left off.

Two of the major contributors to the study of American Indian languages were Franz Boas, a German physicist and geographer turned anthropologist, and Major J. W. Powell of the Bureau of American Ethnology in Washington, D.C. Powell is best known for his classification of American Indian languages which he based on the earlier works of such men as Horatio Hale, James C. Pilling, Stephen Riggs, and J. Owen Dorsey. Powell's task was to classify American Indian languages into similar groupings called language stocks. Although his original work has been revised by a number of linguists over the past twenty years, his early works remain a classic in the field of comparative linguistics.

By comparing vocabularies, Powell classified all American languages into 58 families—larger groupings in which tribal dialects were related but not necessarily mutually intelligible to all members of the language family. Of the 58 families, which have since been reduced, 6 are represented on the Southern Plains.

The largest singular language family of this area in terms of numbers of tribes is the Siouan (not to be confused with the Sioux tribe proper, which is also a member of the family). The Siouan is in turn divided into two major groups: the Dhegiha comprising the Omaha, Osage, Ponca, Kansa, and Quapaw; and the Chiwere, made up of the Oto, Missouri, and Iowa. The second largest family is the Caddoan made up of the Caddo proper, Pawnee Confederacy, and Wichita. The Comanche and Kiowa are both members of the Uto-Aztecan family. Kiowa is unique unto itself although it resembles other languages in the family, but Comanche is interchangeable with Shoshoni, a tribe from the Plateau area which also belongs to the Uto-Aztecan family. Cheyenne and Arapaho are not mutually understandable but are both members of the Algonquian family, which is the largest in the United States and Canada. The Apache and Kiowa Apache are members of the Athabascan family and share a language similar to Navajo. Tonkawan is represented solely by the Tonkawa tribe.

Obviously, with so many tribes speaking a number of dissimilar languages it was difficult to communicate on the Southern Plains. This was partially remedied by the widespread use of Indian sign language—not a very sophisticated means of communication, but convenient for use as a trade language or for expressing very simple ideas.

Unlike the alphabet used by deaf mutes, gestures in sign language did not represent letters of the alphabet (of which there were none), nor did they stand for syllables. Each gesture, like Chinese calligraphy, represented one word. Most gestures in the sign language were very logical and many are similar to gestures non-Indians used to accompany speech when describing motion or height by moving the hands in appropriate directions either slowly or quickly.

Each tribe had a particular designation in sign language based on one of its customs or traditions. The Comanche were known as Snakes, indicated by moving the index finger of the right hand in a zigzag motion drawn toward the body at chest level—much as we would indicate a snake crawling in reverse. The Caddo were known as Pierced Noses from an old custom in which they bored the nose for insertion of a decorative ring. The sign was made by passing the right index finger under the nose. In the old days, the Kiowa warriors cut off their hair over the right ear. The sign for them was made as if clipping the hair in this manner. The sign for the Cheyenne was made by drawing the right index finger across the left index finger several times. The sign may refer to the custom of Cheyenne warriors cutting off the fingers of their slain enemies, or more likely, their habit of using wild turkey to feather their arrows. The sign for Arapaho was Rub Noses, but the reason for this name is unknown. For the Pawnees the sign for Wolf was used.

To give an example of the simplicity of sign language, it is important to point out some of its peculiarities. The same gesture, for example, was used to signify who, what, where, when, why, or how. The gesture might be better translated "Question?"

"Where are you going?" would be "Question you go?" The same signs of course would be used for "When are you going?" or "How are you going?" Therefore one could not rely solely upon phrasing questions as one normally does in speech.

"When are you going?" would become "Are you going now?"

"How are you going?" would be translated "Are you going by horseback?" Therefore in sign language, many answers to questions might be anticipated to make them absolutely clear.

Many signs would be familiar to those who had never encountered Indian sign language. "Up" and "down" were signified by pointing in the respective positions. "High" and "low" were measured with the palm of the hand placed parallel to the ground at whatever height was to be indicated. "Come" was indicated by moving the index finger toward one's chest. "Go" was indicated by the reverse.

Many objects in trade were simply indicated by

pointing to them. Colors were signified by pointing to objects of the color desired.

In addition to sign language, tribes were able to converse through a few Indians who were multilingual. Comanche was also used as a *lingua franca* on the Plains. In my opinion, Comanche would be one of the easiest Indian languages for an English-speaking person to learn because much of the word order in Comanche is similar to English. This is not true of many other Indian languages in which the word order in a sentence seems to be just the opposite of English. Comanche also is noted for using a minimum amount of words to express the maximum number of meanings.

For example, in English we refer to ourselves or our possessions by three different words which are not interchangeable with each other. "I" must be the subject of the sentence; "me" must be the object. "My" signifies possession. In Comanche, only one word *nu* (pronounced roughly as the "no" in "nothing") stands for all three English equivalents depending on where it is placed in the sentence. *Nu tsa tsat* means "I am good." *Nu nani* means "My name." *Nu 'u,* "That's me!"

Comanche also uses the same word *ge* (as the "ge" in "get") for "no!" and "not." When used alone, *ge* simply means "no." When used with a verb it means "not" as in the sentence *genu bekarui*, "It's not going to kill me" (*nu bekarui* means "It's going to kill me"). *Ge* can also be used to negate the positive. *Hin,* for example, means "what," or "something." *Gehin* means "nothing." To the question *Hin a un?* "What do you want?" the answer might be *Gehin nu.* "Nothing (I)."

In describing a person who does something, Comanche has an equivalent to the English "er." *Nuka* means "to dance." *Nukawap* means a "dancer." *Duniqua* means "to sing." *Duniquawap* means a "singer." While we add "s" or "es" to a word to form a plural, the Comanche sometimes double a syllable (called reduplication in linguistics). *Paraibo* means "chief." *Paparaibo* means "chiefs."

When the white man came, bringing along new items such as plows, wagons, trains, things never before seen by the Indian, new words had to be invented to denote these things. Sometimes the Indian described the object. Upon getting their first taste of whiskey from the white traders, the Comanche agreed that it was *bosa ba*—"crazy water" from *bosa*, "crazy," and *ba*, "water." In other cases whole words were borrowed from English or Spanish. Words which are derived from another language and kept intact, with the possible exception of altering the pronunciation, are called loan words. In Comanche, for instance, the words for "bread" (*tawtiya*) and "potatoes" (*piapus*) come from the Spanish *tortilla* and *papas*. The word for "twenty-five cents" is still *duiwits*, a corruption of the English "two bits."

A marvelous example of how a new word undergoes phonetic change to render it more comfortable among the adapters is found among the near neighbors of the Comanche, the Kiowa. In Kiowa there is a sound very peculiar to the language usually written *dl* and pronounced like the "dle" in "middle." *Gyesadl* means "It is hot." *Hodl* means "to kill." *K'awndedl* means "badly." When the Kiowa first saw an automobile, instead of making up a new word or sentence to describe it, they adapted the new English word to fit the phonetics of Kiowa and called it *awdlmodlbidl!*

Just as some will say the quickest way to a man's heart is through his stomach, the quickest way to learning about people of different cultures is through their language. Learning a people's language has always been an integral part of the anthropologist's work. Learning

what people have to say about their own society tells us
how and what they think about things. Virtually every
writer on American Indians has pointed out that curse
words and obscenities are lacking in all Indian languages. The worst that one man could say about another is that he was no good, lazy, or poor in hunting.
Someone might be compared to an animal or a member
of an enemy tribe if any derogatory remark were required. Or one might use a pun, or play on words.

I remember once spending some time with a Caddo
family in Oklahoma. I always made it a practice to learn
at least a few words of each tribe I visited. I had a note-
book and was asking the family how to say a number of
simple expressions in Caddo. One of the first words to
learn, of course, in any language is "friend." The
woman of the family gave me the word when I asked.
"Tesha," she said. Immediately her husband laughed
and told me to pronounce it exactly as his wife had said
because another word *tasha* meant "coyote" and nobody wanted to be called that.

When I asked for the word for "salt," again the man
laughed. In Caddo the word *wedish* means both "salt"
and "show-off," depending on how it is used in the sentence. In Caddo, which is also true of most American
Indian languages, there is an absence of the sounds "f"
and "v." The Caddo word for "coffee" is also a loan
word pronounced *kah-bee.*

The word "how," so often heard in movies as an Indian greeting, is widely used on the Southern Plains. It
is pronounced somewhat differently from one tribe to
another and is usually followed by the word for friend.
Here are some ways in which the expression is used by a
few of the Southern Plains tribes. The samples are written in the English phonetic equivalent and mean
"Greetings!" or "Hello!"

Caddo—*Hoh tayshah*
Comanche—*Hahn haints*
Kiowa—*Haw nawkohnm*
Osage—*Hohway*
Oto—*How Intahroh*
Omaha—*How kageha*
Ponca—*How kageha*
Quapaw—*Hohway*

While most American Indian languages are still considered preliterate, North America has proved to be a bonanza for students of linguistics. There are many Indian languages that are written and used in their written form, such as Navajo and Sioux. Some languages have not yet been analyzed. But there are hundreds of languages spoken by Indians within a limited geographic area, and so today these languages are the object of much study.

Franz Boas, the pioneer in this field, noted some important reactions by Indians whose languages he investigated. First he found that if he could teach an Indian an alphabet, no matter how approximate to the actual sounds of the native dialect, the Indian was capable of automatically breaking his language down into words when writing it. No matter how preliterate, the Indian was aware of the functions of grammar whether or not he had a written language. This was one of the major discoveries in showing how sophisticated Indian languages really are. At the same time it disproved any suggestions that Indian languages were primitive in the literal sense.

Secondly, Boas found to his amazement that when he himself was able to formulate an alphabet for a given language and take down dictation, the Indians believed he was capable of *speaking* their language when he read the dictations back to them. Other fieldworkers found this to be true also. The white man's magic of writing somehow gave them a mysterious, overnight comprehension of a language foreign to them only hours before.

For the most part, in recording Indian texts Boas and others who followed him used the international phonetic alphabet—an alphabet made up of a number of Latin and Greek letters augmented by diacritical marks enabling the linguist to write any sound in the languages of the world. But others, using only English letters, created alphabets—and later dictionaries and grammars. Although there are many highly technical studies of American Indian languages, there are a few related to Indians of the Southern Plains which, with some effort, can be read by interested students. Some outstanding works on Indian languages (listed by tribe) are :

Arapaho—*Arapaho Dialects*, A. L. Kroeber, 1916.

Caddo—*Vocabulary of the Caddoquis or Caddo Language*, J. Sibley, 1879.

Cheyenne—*Cheyenne Grammar* (1952) and *English-Cheyenne Dictionary* (1913), R. C. Petter.

Comanche—*Comanche Texts*, E. D. Canonge, 1958, and *Vocabulario del idioma comanche*, Garcia Rejon, n.d.

Iowa—*Descriptive Grammar of Ioway-Oto*, W. Whitman, 1947.

Kiowa—*Vocabulary of the Kiowa Language*, J. P. Harrington, 1928.

Omaha—*The Cegiha Language*, J. Owen Dorsey, 1890.

Osage—*A Dictionary of the Osage Language*, F. La-Flesche, 1932.

Pawnee—*Caddoan Texts: Pawnee*, G. Weltfish, 1937.

Ponca—*Notes on the Ponka Grammar*, F. Boas, 1906.

13

Pan-Indianism

ROBERT K. THOMAS, a Cherokee anthropologist living in Oklahoma, once defined Pan-Indianism as "an attempt to create a new ethnic group, the American Indian."

This may come as a surprise to those who have always considered the American Indian a nationality. The truth, however, is that there never has been such a group, culturally or historically.

It has been estimated that before Columbus arrived there were as many as two thousand separate tribal groups. After the arrival of the white man, the number of tribes began to decrease, some became extinct, other smaller bands fused with larger tribes for self-protection, as in the case of the Kiowa Apache with the Kiowa. Although over the years there were attempts to unify tribes, these attempts failed for the most part, mainly because of the separateness and individuality of the Indian. Even today, when asked, "Who are you?" most will respond "Comanche" (or whatever tribe). Next in order of importance, the usual Indian considers himself

Indian, and, finally, *American*. In short, the Indian's first allegiance is to his tribe.

As we have seen in earlier chapters, even in an area the size of the Southern Plains, there was a great deal of diversity in language, religion, tribal dress, and customs. Until their relocation to Indian Territory, many tribes never even heard of others who were destined to become their neighbors. Although the exchange of ideas between some tribes had been going on long before the white man came, the incorporation of one tribal trait by another became more escalated after the Indian had been forcibly removed from his original home and required to live on a reservation.

Because more singularly large tribes, ones from entirely different kinds of original homelands, were removed to Oklahoma, this state is often given credit as being the cradle of Pan-Indianism. In other words, those traits which had originally been Comanche, Cheyenne, Kiowa, or Apache began to merge into that which could be commonly called Indian.

Although students of the American Indian were not sure what direction Pan-Indianism was going, the term began to be applied to almost any cultural event in which more than one tribe participated. Thus at inter-tribal ceremonials like the fair or at some of the smaller powwows, songs, dances, and dance costumes in particular were referred to as Pan-Indian, with little regard to where the songs, dances, and costumes had their origin.

Even in religion, Peyotism was being called the religious branch of Pan-Indianism. In the area of civil rights, organizations like the National Congress of American Indians (NCAI), sometimes called the United Nations of Indian tribes, and the National Indian Youth Council (NIYC) were becoming the political force of Pan-Indianism. Real Pan-Indianism emerged noticeably in the area of civil rights. Indians all over the nation realized that they had to unify in order to form voting blocks, lobby in Washington, and fight together for those things which were denied the American Indian, mainly, his right to choose his own destiny and not simply become assimilated into the dominant white society of America.

The Indian, therefore, has been attempting to form a national, concentrated effort to introduce legislation into Congress which will give him equality under his own terms. He wants to challenge the abrogation of hundreds of treaties which have left the Indian landless in many cases, the most poverty-stricken of all minority groups, and with alarming rates of alcoholism, suicide, and delinquency which far exceed the national average. The American Indian is not happy with the legacy carved out for him by the white man, and today he is doing something about it.

Many experts are inclined to look at Pan-Indianism as an eventual absorption of many tribal customs and philosophies into one super Indian race. At the same time Indians themselves are demanding the right to follow their own *tribal* customs—even though today it is impossible to distinguish such things as dance, costumes, songs, and the like in the dance arena. Some Indians are insisting that education on reservations be conducted in the child's native language—not English. This is especially true on larger reservations where there is less contact with English-speaking people.

In the mid-fifties, Oklahoma Pan-Indianism overspilled its boundaries. The Oklahoma style of dancing and costumes began to be popular on reservations located a great distance from the state. Such formalities as the war dance contest, the powwow princess, and fancy dance costumes began to appear even on the Northern High Plains and Plateau as well as in urban centers around the country where Indians had been relocated. A strange kind of revivalism began to take place in Oklahoma where it had all started. At the same time that anthropologists were reporting the Pan-Indian movement, tribes in Oklahoma such as the Kiowa, Kiowa Apache, and Ponca were beginning to revive customs, songs, and dances which were irrevocably tribal.

What had happened to the move toward assimilation? The Kiowa reinstated their Black Legging Society for their tribal veterans of foreign wars. The Kiowa Gourd Dance Clan became even more active. The Kiowa Apache followed with the reorganization of the Black Feet Society. The Ponca became interested again in the old Hedushka Society. The tribes still fought for equal rights by collaborating with each other through representation in national organizations. But with equal vigor they began to reestablish things that were tribally oriented.

Although Oklahoma can with certainty be called the cradle of Pan-Indianism, the movement spread rapidly among all tribes, with particular emphasis on civil rights. While the term "Pan-Indian" is still used by anthropologists to point out certain similarities in surviving customs, it has been replaced in the 1960's by a more powerful term—"Red Power"!

Vine Deloria, Jr., a Standing Rock Sioux and former executive director of the National Congress of American Indians, coined the word. Another Indian, Clyde Warrior, a Ponca from Oklahoma, was instrumental in challenging the status quo in Indian affairs, asking for reforms in Indian policy.

As a member of the board of directors of the National

Indian Youth Council, an organization representing individual Indians rather than whole tribes, Warrior led the first fish-in in the state of Washington. This was in protest of a state law which prohibited Indians from fishing in waters where they had fished for hundreds of years and which by treaty were still rightfully theirs. Warrior was outspoken in challenging not only the white man but other Indians who he felt had sold out to the dominant society. He had been pushed to the edge after seeing his elders stripped of their dignity and his people forced to live by the rules and regulations of bureaucrats. He called for the National Indian Youth Council to help Indians reassert themselves. Writing in the council's official organ, *Americans Before Columbus,* he said:

> The National Indian Youth Council must introduce to this sick room of stench and anonymity some fresh air of new Indianness. A fresh air of new honesty and integrity, a fresh air of new Indian idealism, a fresh air of a new Great Indian America.

The sickroom he referred to was the present condition of the Indian in America: an average life-span of forty-five years, an average income of $1,500 per year, the worst living conditions of any minority group, a suicide rate that was three times the national average and, on some reservations, ten times. But most of all he decried the indignity of the American Indian who never had been allowed the right to voice an opinion in the handling of his own destiny.

Although Warrior died from the white man's alcohol, others took up the movement. It has grown rapidly throughout the past decade, taking the form of demonstrations, take-overs of unclaimed land, and a barrage of communications designed to keep the nation apprised of the Indian movement and the people's fight for self-determination.

It is common in the West to see signs and bumper stickers on Indian cars which proclaim INDIAN POWER, THINK INDIAN, IF UR INDIAN UR IN, and CUSTER DIED FOR YOUR SINS, the latter of which became the title of a book by Vine Deloria, Jr., which lashed out at the mistreatment of Indian people. When itinerant hippies invaded many reservations to go native, another sign bore the inscription HIPPIES AND HOPIS DON'T MIX.

There are a number of publications headed by all-Indian staffs which circulate news nationally. One of the leaders in providing general information is the *Indian Historian* published by the American Indian Historical Society under the direction of Rupert Costo, chairman of the Cahuilla tribe. While owned by Indians, many contributors to this publication are well-known anthropologists and historians, Indian and non-Indian. The National Congress of American Indians publishes the *Indian Sentinel*, and the National Indian Youth Council, *Americans Before Columbus*. One of the most interesting and newest publications is called *Akwesasne Notes*. It reproduces news stories and editorials from many sources concerning American Indians and is distributed free of charge to nearly ten thousand people.

The most dramatic show of Red Power occurred on November 20, 1969, when a group of Indians landed on Alcatraz, an island located in San Francisco Bay. Although the Indian occupation was called illegal, the Indians argued that, according to a treaty between the United States government and the Sioux Indians in 1868 which provided for unused federal land to revert to the Indians, Alcatraz was legally theirs. Since Alcatraz had been abandoned for many years because it was too expensive to maintain, the Indians took the opportunity to put the treaty to the test. Since they occupied the "Rock," legislation has been introduced to let them stay there. The twentieth-century Indian attack also won wide support from all segments of society, including some members of Congress.

Monroe E. Price, professor of law at UCLA and deputy director of California Indian Legal Services, said of the invasion: "The taking of Alcatraz may begin a new era of Pan-Indian awareness and activity. The hard and lonely settlement has been greeted not with tear gas but with a sense of hope and promise. The band of Indians on the prison island have formed a policy for themselves and by themselves. They are staking a claim for the restoration of a culture and a strength of community that should not be lost. The wager they are asking the country to make is a safe one: that they cannot be more wrong than the great white fathers of the past."

Hard and lonely settlement it is! There is no heat or water. All supplies must be taken out to the Indian people by boat. Yet they are determined to stay.

One Indian on the Rock described it succinctly: "Alcatraz is a rocky, isolated, nonproductive small island. It is very much like a typical Indian reservation."

The Indians living there have as their greatest enemy boredom. But they have started a school for children, a cultural center, and even broadcast a radio show from the island. Their biggest concern is having a place where Indian culture may be taught and retained.

Richard Oakes, a Mohawk Indian on Alcatraz, expressed his feelings: "There's sad neglect of all the different tribal cultures. Ten years from now, there may not be anybody out on the reservation to retain our culture and be able to relate it. So this is actually a move, not so much to liberate the island, but to liberate ourselves for the sake of cultural survival."

The Indians on Alcatraz call themselves Indians of All Tribes, a further development in the concept of Pan-Indianism. A young Indian girl on the island said: "When we claimed Alcatraz island for Indians of all tribes, we meant exactly that. It's so very important for the Indian people to realize that we're never going to get the island unless the Indian people are going to come here and represent the Indians of all tribes. We need to have Indian people that know the Indian culture, to begin now teaching it to the younger people here on Alcatraz."

The fate of Alcatraz and all that it means to the Indian people at this writing is being determined by Congress. On December 23, 1969, the following joint resolution was introduced into the House of Representatives:

> *Resolved by the Senate and the House of Representatives of the United States of America assembled*, That the President of the United States is directed to initiate immediate negotiations with delegated representatives of the Alcatraz Relief Fund and any other appropriate representatives of the American Indian community with the objective of transferring unencumbered title in fee of Alcatraz Island to the Alcatraz Relief Fund or any other designated organization of the American Indian community.

The Indians, somewhat fearful that the democratic process may prove to be fatal to their attempts at what they consider real democracy, have made appeals to all segments of American society to support their right to retain Alcatraz by writing to their Congressmen.

But demonstrations are not the only method being used to fight the injustices to the Indian. Because of their relatively small number, the Indians must work within the legal system of the United States. It is not unusual, then, to find many young Indian students following a career in law.

Recently at a convocation of American Indian scholars, the first ever to be held, nearly two hundred Indians met at Princeton University to raise critical questions concerning the destiny of their people. Self-determination, the right to make decisions for themselves regarding tribal policy, was keynote in the daily discussions. The importance of retaining Indian culture, religion, philosophy, language, and arts was discussed. But this group, in addition to its scholarship, had a determination to give their own people Indian leadership that exemplified itself in a spirit of courage.

One Osage lawyer who attended the gathering told me, "I've fought in the Marines, I've fought in the bars, and I've fought in the jails. Now all I want to do is fight, but I want to do it in a court of law. And I don't care what I have to fight about—land rights, water rights, natural resources—anything for the benefit of my people. Just give me a good fight."

Before Clyde Warrior died, he said, "Let's raise some hell."

It appears that Alcatraz is the first rung in the ladder to human rights for American Indians. Warrior's words have been heeded. Red Power has just begun.

14

Americans First and Lasting

I ONCE read in a high school history book the following question and answer at the end of a chapter on westward expansion:

Question: What did the white man do for the Indian in exchange for taking his land?

Answer: The white man named cities, states, and rivers after the Indian.

That this kind of naïveté abounds in history books is another of the many ways in which the general American public has evaded the real issues in American Indian affairs. Most will agree that the Indian got a raw deal without realizing that the Indian still continues to get a raw deal to this very day. Some history books also say that the Indians made treaties with the United States government and "ceded" their lands, as if it were some kind of voluntary act or that the Indian had any alternative. But then the history books also say that Columbus (or Leif Ericson) discovered America, a statement that makes today's Indian flinch. For he knows well that Indians discovered America! Twenty-five thousand years of residency on the North American continent certainly qualifies the Indian as the first one here. After all, the Indians say, it was just poor navigation that led Columbus to the New World. Even the word "Indian" was a mistake! To the statement that the Pilgrims landed on Plymouth Rock, the Indian responds, "Too bad the rock didn't land on them!"

While white Americans think the Indian wars are over, history itself presents in the strongest language a series of horrifying, conspiratorial, deceitful events that were well planned to annihilate the first Americans. And the Indians truly believe that the sequence has not ended.

What some history books do not describe is that many Indian tribes were forcibly removed from their homes and marched under the severest conditions to strange territories, which they came to regard as concentration camps. The whites called them reservations.

After signing treaties with the Indians, the United States broke many of them—and continues to break them. Through the calculated planning of U.S. generals, the buffalo, the prime source of food, clothing, and shelter for the Plains tribes, were methodically destroyed in order to cut off the Indians' very means of subsistence. On some reservations where Indians were freezing to death because of little clothing and poor shelter, blankets sent directly from hospitals in which patients were dying from smallpox and other diseases were used to comfort—and kill—helpless men, women, and children. After having reduced the Indians to one quarter of their original population, the United States then decided to take care of the first Americans by establishing the Bureau of Indian Affairs in Washington, D.C. Originally, Indian affairs had come under the jurisdiction of the War Department. In 1849, the bureau was shifted to the newly created Department of Interior where it remains today.

In 1887, the Dawes Act, sometimes called the Indian

Allotment Act, was enacted by Congress, and some of the land comprising reservations was allotted to individual Indians. The Dawes Act had a particularly strong effect on the Indians living in Oklahoma. Beginning in 1887 and continuing through 1901, all reservations were abolished in Oklahoma. The land was allotted separately to individuals, and surplus land once belonging to the tribes was opened up to white men. The Kiowa-Comanche and Wichita-Caddo reservations were the last to go—over 3,000,000 acres. Along with the land went the mineral rights, with the exception of the Osage country where the tribe retained the subsurface mineral rights. Coincidentally, in Oklahoma, "mineral" in the main is synonymous with "oil."

Thus after land allotment, the Indian tribes living in Oklahoma became clustered in small communities rather than on large reservations. Today one can drive through the rolling Prairies and never know when one is in Indian Territory. But one can safely guess that when he passes the monstrous oil wells pumping away millions of dollars of wealth each year, chances are the wells are *not* on Indian land.

On June 2, 1924, the Congress of the United States conferred citizenship on all Indians. It seems that was the least they could do for people living here for thousands of years, but until that time only a few Indians had been regarded as full citizens of the United States. Not until 1948, however, were all Indians eligible to vote. In a few states Indians had been disenfranchised by individual interpretations of state constitutions until these interpretations were finally ruled unconstitutional.

In 1934, under the Indian Reorganization Act, individual tribes were given the power to develop their own administrative policies and, theoretically, govern themselves. The Cheyenne and Arapaho, for example, incorporated as the Cheyenne-Arapaho Tribes of Oklahoma, governed by a business committee elected every two years by popular vote. The Caddo are incorporated as the Caddo Indian Tribe of Oklahoma. The confederated bands of the Pawnee are incorporated as the Pawnee Indian Tribe of Oklahoma and are administered by a business council made up of the chieftains of the four Pawnee bands. The Kiowa, Comanche, and Apache are represented by the Kiowa-Comanche-Apache Intertribal Business Committee whose members are elected every four years.

Despite the abolition of reservations in Oklahoma and the Congressional act designed to give Indians the power to govern themselves, the Bureau of Indian Affairs still maintains field offices in eleven Oklahoma towns, each manned by a representative of the bureau and a staff. While the Indians theoretically govern themselves, there is little they can do without the official sanction of the field office and the home office of the bureau. Many Indians therefore know they cannot really make their own decisions. Ultimately, it is still the white man who oversees the day-to-day activities of the Indian.

In addition to the field offices, the Bureau of Indian Affairs operates Indian schools in Oklahoma. The area of education is ranked foremost in the minds of Indians. They believe that their children should certainly have the right to be educated in order to carry on the unfinished battle of Indian equality. Yet the bureau schools, according to the Indian people, leave much to be desired. A recent report was more specific about school conditions in general and told of the shocking reality of Indian education.

Although the bureau operates 77 boarding schools

and 147 day schools, over 57 percent of all Indian children are sent to public schools where they must generally learn in an atmosphere of hate and prejudice. About 35,000 Indian children attend boarding schools, while less than half go to day schools. In 1966, the shocking fact was that 16,000 Indian children of school age were not attending any school at all. Those who did became a part of a statistic that shows the average educational level of the American Indian as fifth grade with an annual drop-out rate twice the national average. Another hard fact is that in addition to being behind in education at the grade level, the longer the Indian child remained in school, the farther behind he fell.

There are a number of reasons why education becomes a horror for the Indian child. To begin, the boarding school child must not only leave his parents, but in many cases must travel great distances to school. Some Oklahoma schools run by the government have students from as far away as Alaska—a 6,000-mile journey into a strange and different kind of country. Both parents and child suffer from the separation, causing undue stress on the child, who is somehow supposed to relate to the education system at any cost.

Bureau schools usually lack good facilities and often have a white teaching staff that fails to appreciate Indian culture and is ready to dismiss things of value to the Indian as being primitive and wrong. The Indian student is frequently taught that he should be ashamed to be an Indian, that he should give up the heathen religion of his forefathers, the language of his tribe. In public schools he often reads from books that have little good to say about Indians. Soon the young Indian child begins to realize just how he and his parents are considered by whites. He feels the gnawing of prejudice from both classmates and teachers. The adolescent Indian has little opportunity to complete his education in an atmosphere of shame and indignation. He retires from a healthy, active life. He rejects the values of the whites. He drops out.

No people can live under these conditions for long without entering into some sort of protest. The very lives of the American Indian are being challenged just as surely as they were threatened in the mid-nineteenth century. Alcoholism, suicide, diseases no longer considered a threat to the white community—all these plus the total dehumanization of the Indian from the time he enters school until the time he drops out of society—can do nothing but leave an indelible imprint of hate on the American Indian.

There is no question that he was the first American. Some people have argued that he is vanishing, that is, although he is increasing in numbers, he will in time become assimilated into the mainstream of white society. To assist him in his entry into the American way of life, the Bureau of Indian Affairs has dedicated its service. But the Indian no longer accepts white values as the end in itself. The Indian is tenacious; he does not want to give up the Indian way of life. He wants his culture to be lasting.

Some will argue that too much fuss is being made over such a small minority. Some will say that this minority is destined to melt into the white man's world. But the fact that such a small group of people can hold onto their own values, their own culture, against all odds from the supersociety, makes the American Indian as immovable as the very rock of Alcatraz. Over three hundred years of deprivation have served only to strengthen the Indian way. Americans, first and lasting, the Indians will fight to retain their right to self-assertion and self-determination.

Bibliography

Akwesasne Notes, a monthly newspaper of current Indian affairs. Middletown, Connecticut, Wesleyan University.

American Indian Crafts and Culture, a monthly magazine, PO Box 3538, Tulsa, Oklahoma.

BERTHRONG, DONALD J., *The Southern Cheyennes.* Norman, University of Oklahoma, 1963.

CURTIS, NATALIE, *The Indians' Book.* New York, Dover, 1968.

DELORIA, VINE, JR., *Custer Died for Your Sins.* New York, Macmillan, 1969.

DENSMORE, FRANCES, *Pawnee Music.* Bureau of American Ethnology, Bulletin 93. Washington, D.C., Government Printing Office, 1929.

———, *Cheyenne and Arapaho Music.* Los Angeles, Southwest Museum, 1936.

DORSEY, J. OWEN, "A Study of Siouan Cults." Eleventh Annual Report, Bureau of American Ethnology. Washington, D.C., Government Printing Office, 1890.

———, *Omaha and Ponka Letters.* Washington, D.C., Government Printing Office, 1891.

DRIVER, HAROLD E., *Indians of North America.* Chicago, University of Chicago, 1961.

FLETCHER, ALICE C., "The Hako: A Pawnee Ceremony." Twenty-second Annual Report, Bureau of American Ethnology. Washington, D.C., Government Printing Office, 1904.

———, and LaFLESCHE, F., "The Omaha Tribe." Twenty-eighth Annual Report, Bureau of American Ethnology. Washington, D.C., Government Printing Office, 1906.

GRINNELL, GEORGE BIRD, *The Cheyenne Indians.* New York, Cooper Square, 1923.

———, *Pawnee Hero Stories and Folk Tales.* Lincoln, University of Nebraska, 1961.

———, *The Fighting Cheyennes.* Norman, University of Oklahoma, 1964.

HOEBEL, E. ADAMSON, *Comanches, Lords of the Southern Plains.* Norman, University of Oklahoma, 1964.

HOWARD, JAMES H., *The Ponca.* Bureau of American Ethnology, Bulletin 195. Washington, D.C., Government Printing Office, 1965.

JONES, DOUGLAS C., *The Treaty of Medicine Lodge.* Norman, University of Oklahoma, 1966.

LaBARRE, WESTON, *The Peyote Cult.* New Haven, Connecticut, The Shoe String Press, 1964.

LAUBIN, REGINALD and GLADYS, *The Indian Tipi.* Norman, University of Oklahoma, 1964.

LINTON, RALPH, *The Thunder Ceremony of the Pawnee*. Chicago, Field Museum of Natural History, 1922.

LOWIE, ROBERT H., *Societies of the Kiowa*. New York, American Museum of Natural History, 1916.

————, *Indians of the Plains*. New York, American Museum of Natural History, 1954.

MARRIOTT, ALICE, *The Ten Grandmothers*. Norman, University of Oklahoma, 1945.

————, *Saynday's People: The Kiowa Indians and the Stories They Told*. Lincoln, University of Nebraska, 1963.

MATHEWS, JOHN JOSEPH, *The Osages, Children of the Middle Waters*. Norman, University of Oklahoma, 1961.

MAYHALL, MILDRED P., *The Kiowas*. Norman, University of Oklahoma, 1962.

MCALLESTER, DAVID P., *Peyote Music*. New York, Viking Fund Publications, 1949.

MOONEY, JAMES, "Calendar History of the Kiowa." Seventeenth Annual Report, Bureau of American Ethnology. Washington, D.C., Government Printing Office, 1898.

————, *Kiowa-Apache*. Bureau of American Ethnology, Bulletin 30. Washington, D.C., Government Printing Office, 1907.

————, *Wichita*. Bureau of American Ethnology, Bulletin 30. Washington, D.C., Government Printing Office, 1910.

————, *Ghost-Dance Religion and the Sioux Outbreak of 1890*. Chicago, University of Chicago, 1965.

MURIE, JAMES R., *Pawnee Indian Societies*. New York, American Museum of Natural History, 1914.

POWERS, WILLIAM K., *Indian Dancing and Costumes*. New York, G. P. Putnam's, 1966.

————, *Indians of the Northern Plains*. New York, G. P. Putnam's, 1969.

ROE, FRANK GILBERT, *The Indian and the Horse*. Norman, University of Oklahoma, 1962.

SANDOZ, MARI, *Cheyenne Autumn*. New York, Hastings House, 1953.

SCHMITT, MARTIN F., and BROWN, DEE, *Fighting Indians of the West*. New York, Scribner's, 1955.

SKINNER, ALANSON, *Societies of the Iowa, Kansa, and Ponca Indians*. New York, American Museum of Natural History, 1915.

SPIER, LESLIE, *Notes on the Kiowa Sun Dance*. New York, American Museum of Natural History, 1921.

STEINER, STAN, *The New Indians*. New York, Harper and Row, 1968.

WELLMAN, PAUL I., *The Indian Wars of the West*. Garden City, Doubleday, 1954.

WRIGHT, MURIEL H., *A Guide to the Indian Tribes of Oklahoma*. Norman, University of Oklahoma, 1965.

Index

The Author

William K. Powers is the author of two popular and critically praised books from Putnam's—*Indians of the Northern Plains* and *Here Is Your Hobby: Indian Dancing and Costumes.* For more than twenty years Mr. Powers has been a student of Indian culture, specializing in tribes of the Great Plains. Several years ago he was adopted by the Sioux at Pine Ridge, South Dakota, and he speaks Sioux fluently. A resident of Kendall Park, New Jersey, Mr. Powers, his wife and sons follow the Indian powwow circuit each summer.